Eccentric Cambridge

the Bradt City Guide

Benedict le Vay

www.bradtguides.com

Bradt Travel Guides Ltd, UK
The Globe Pequot Press Inc, USA

· edition ·

I

Have Cambridge students got something against Austin cars? This one was left dangling over the river from the Bridge of Sighs

(CEN) page 231

The Middle Ages weren't all crude, lewd and rude, but they were funny, as this detail from the superb Macclesfield Psalter, a Pythonesque national treasure at the Fitzwilliam Museum, suggests (FM) page 172

Richard Collins, the nude Cambridge cyclist had one naked ambition – to ride right through the city starkers

(CEN) page 4

Bin there, done that:
Charlie Cavey, the Cambridge busker

.(AB/Alamy) page 48

Gargoyles abound in Cambridge. This one is, strictly, a grotesque (FS)

Settling a 450-year-old grudge: Magdalene College recently used this ugly gargoyle to gets its revenge on a banker from the 1570s; he will now dribble forever into the Cam (BV)

Clare Bridge had a wedge cut out of one of its balls, supposedly because the builder's pay was a shilling short (RB) page 73

is HOUSE is dedicated to those spl..d
..LLOWS who make DRINKING a pleasu..
..o reach CONTENTMENT before CAPACI..
..d who, whatever the DRINK, can tak..
..hold it, enjoy it and STILL remain
GENTLEMEN

THE KING STREET RUN

Ale to our heroes:
Cambridge pubs
include a plaque
to the DNA
discoverers at
the Eagle;
a notice about
gentlemen who
believe in
moderation at
the Champion of
the Thames;
and, close by, a pub
celebrating those
who don't,
The King Street Run
(BV), (RB), (BV)
pages 143/145/144

CHAMPION OF THE THAMES

DNA Double Helix 1953
"The secret of life"
For decades the Eagle was the local
pub for scientists from the nearby
Cavendish Laboratory.
It was here on February 28th 1953 that
Francis Crick and James Watson first
announced their discovery of how
DNA carries genetic information.
Unveiled by James Watson
25th April 2003

As it is supposed to be done:
punting under the Bridge of Sighs

(RB) page 182

Moving in religious circles: Cambridge's beautiful Round Church is one of only four in England (RB) page 207

SIC TRANSIT GLORIA MUNDI

GVLIELMVS SPARROW GENNATVS AN 1641 ÆTATIS SVÆ 88

The going's turf: the grass maze at Hilton was crawled around on hands and knees as part of a religious tradition (MD) page 215

Author/Acknowledgements

AUTHOR

Benedict le Vay is a national newspaper sub-editor who has worked in four continents but wrote his first book, *Eccentric Britain*, more or less by accident after collecting oddities about his home country. He says he was 'staggered' by the response, which includes media attention from the *Shetland Times* to Gulf Radio, and publicity tours in America and New Zealand. He describes himself as a frankly rather ordinary, happily married father of two, and is hard-pressed to think of anything eccentric about himself. 'At a push, I'd say, yes, I'm Honorary Secretary of the Friends of A272, and I've asked for my ashes to be blasted from the chimney of my favourite steam locomotive at my funeral. Hasn't everybody?'

ACKNOWLEDGEMENTS

Chris Jakes, Andy Gregory, Matthew Oates, Martin le Vay, Bill Smith, Professor David Matless, Jayme Bryla, Rebecca Attwood. Any mistakes, however, are my own.

First published December 2006
Bradt Travel Guides Ltd
23 High Street, Chalfont St Peter, Bucks SL9 9QE, England; www.bradtguides.com
Published in the US by The Globe Pequot Press Inc,
246 Goose Lane, PO Box 480, Guilford, Connecticut 06437-0480

Text copyright © 2006 Benedict le Vay
Maps copyright © 2006 Bradt Travel Guides Ltd
Based upon Ordnance Survey material by permission of OS on behalf of the controller of Her Majesty's
stationery office © Crown copyright 100046434
Illustrations © Individual photographers and artists (see below)

British Library Cataloguing in Publication Data
A catalogue record for this book is available from the British Library
ISBN-10: 1 84162 172 2   ISBN-13: 978 1 84162 172 2

Photographs Alistair Balderstone/Alamy (AB/Alamy), Ben le Vay (BV), *Cambridge Evening News* (CEN),
Fitzwilliam Museum (FM), Felicity Stanbridge (FS), Michel Duijves (MD), Ryan Barnes (RB)
Front cover Snowy Farr (AB/Alamy) *Title page* Naked cyclist (CEN), Champion of the Thames pub (BV)
Maps Alan Whitaker   **Illustrations** Dave Colton, www.cartoonist.net
Typeset from the author's disc by Wakewing   Printed and bound in Italy by Grafo, Trento

Contents

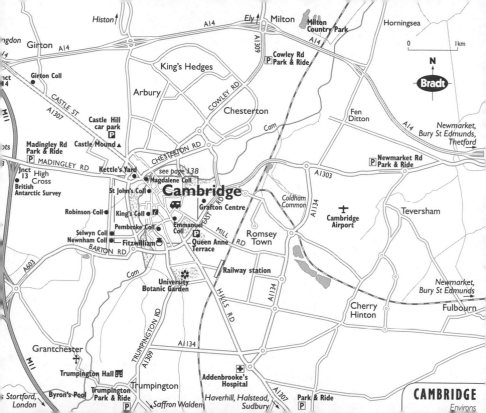

Introduction

WHAT DOES ECCENTRIC MEAN? KNOWING THE DRILL

You might expect this book to start off with spires, historic colleges, begowned dons, punting and the tulip-filled Backs (of the colleges). All of that is utterly marvellous, of course, and will be attended to diligently in due course, but let's instead talk about drilling.

In 2005, had you Googled 'eccentric and Cambridge' the very first entry was some firm selling drills that can operate off centre. This is worth mentioning because eccentric doesn't necessarily mean crackers, oddball, bonkers, lovable, creative, evil, twisted. Those are all judgements that can be applied to some eccentrics, true, but like the drill it means what the Latin origin means – out of centre, away from the middle. By extension fringy, abnormal, not run-of-the-mill. Eccentric people aren't necessarily cuddly, amusing or pleasant, although they can be. There have been eccentric Cambridge-area aristocrats and publicans in our own time, for example, who were evil, rude, cruel and selfish as well as those who were amiable and daftly whimsical.

At the risk of losing those not mechanically minded (who should skip a paragraph), the engineering connection is illuminating. If you are old enough, you'll remember when small boys rushed about tooting and chuffing and pretending to be steam engines (you may even have done this yourself, and feel free to start again now). Their arms would be whirling round beside them in a push-pull motion as if their hands were attached to the edge of a spinning wheel. This is indeed how a back and forth piston can power a rotating wheel, and where the hands connected to the invisible wheel, or in reality the connecting rod to the real wheel, is called by engineers 'the eccentric'. In fact, if your mobile phone has the ability to vibrate in that buzzy way, it's because of an eccentric. A small brass weight is attached to a motor off centre, so the thing dances around the table like a demented hornet.

So 'eccentric' carries no judgement or moral value, it just means not in the real centre. It may be eccentric to mention this in a book about Cambridge, but it is for you to say if this is bonkers, doolally, off-the-wall, barking, amusing, odd or crackers. Those are *judgements*. Eccentricity is just a fact.

THE UNIVERSITY THAT DOESN'T EXIST AND THE COLLEGE SYSTEM

Talking of eccentrics, Cambridge is the home of great logicians where you come up on the down train and get sent down on the up; where Peas Hill is nothing to do with Peas and is flat as a pancake; where great care is taken to obtain exactly the right kind of hood to wear but it is never worn and people who actually do so are sneered at; where May Week is in June, and where in degree exams Pass really means fail, where an ordinary degree is extraordinary, where lower second means third class, and a bachelor can be a woman or a married person.

But then the university itself doesn't really exist. You can't board a taxi at the railway station and ask for the 'University'. Try it. Where would you go? They wouldn't know what you're talking about because it doesn't physically exist (any more than Cambridge Cathedral, which is another story). Undergraduates don't join the university, they join a college, an autonomous ancient corporation which co-operates with other colleges in certain ways. Your loyalty is first and foremost, and lifelong in most cases, to your college. Cambridge is a collection of colleges, and herein lies its strength.

The strength of the British Army is its regiment system where the loyalty is intense, and your enemy – most of the time – is the other regiments. Actually contemplating the intricate structures of Cambridge University I'm reminded more of an RAF type wryly describing the Lancaster bomber as '20,000 rivets flying in close formation'. Cambridge institutions are separate and all have their own pilots, but they do fly in formation. Mostly.

Basically, the university as a whole organises lectures and exams, while the colleges provide teaching of individuals. This can be supervision, a group of three or so students and a don, and also tutorials, which are one-to-one meetings where the students' pastoral, personal and academic progress can all be nurtured. This is Cambridge's, and Oxford's, great strength. This is what makes it one of the top three universities in the world, and a damn beautiful and brilliant one too.

LIST OF MAPS

Eccentric History
Cambridge: history and mystery

Fans of another grand old English university town – the one sometimes derided by Cambridge men as 'a car factory with a Latin quarter attached' – have sometimes characterised Cambridge as a bunch of crumbling buildings set in the middle of the fens, suitable for swamp dwellers who were rejected by Oxford.

Contentious stuff. For one thing, Cambridge never was in the middle of the fens (the impenetrable marshes that once extended northwest of here) but on the edge of them. It was where the Roman road system met the rivers that the Danes could use as their highways, and gave access to the then Isle of Ely. A transport interchange of the Dark Ages, as it were. For another thing, while some early scholars who came to Cambridge did indeed come from Oxford, it was they who rejected that city, not vice versa. As for the strange fen-dwelling people of legend with their webbed feet and dark, devilish ways, well, the history of Cambridge is perhaps even stranger than the popular legend.

GRANTCHESTER PEDIGREE, OR JUST MUDDY SWAMP DWELLERS?

As 'any fule kno', as the great British schoolboy Molesworth always put it, a place name ending *chester* in Britain indicates a Roman town or fort. Thus the *Via Devana*, the Roman road whose straight southeast to northwest route still bisects modern Cambridge (going up Bridge Street to Castle Hill), went from Col*chester* to Godman*chester*, Leicester and on to *Chester* (the name of the military road meant Chester Road, the Latin for Chester being Deva). Although the Romans stopped repairing this strategic highway in AD407, a glance at a map will show the A14 racing northwest from Cambridge on the exact straight line that the legions once trudged behind their imperial eagle standards.

The *Via Devana* would have been the only dry route from East Anglia to the Midlands and the North, and the route to London and the West from Cambridge would have been down the west bank of the Cam. In Cambridge, at around where Castle Hill now is, was the *Via Devana's* crossing with another ancient highway, from north Norfolk to the River Severn. The crossroads is still there.

The river gave access to the sea and to the Isle of Ely, so Cambridge was well sited. Here was firm, dry ground where a settlement could be built, for it was not the middle of a fen.

As the river was then called the Granta, it is logical to believe that any Roman settlement would be known by the early English as Grant*chester*, a particularly tempting concept as there is indeed a village of that name a couple of miles southeast of today's city. This romantic notion has been happily adopted by many, and Grantchester immortalised in honey-soaked homesickness by poet Rupert Brooke.

The truth is more prosaic. Granta meant muddy, which the river still is, and the records show Grenteseta as that village's former name, the ending not meaning anything Roman at all but 'dwellers', in which case any Oxford jibes about mud-dwellers wouldn't have been far off the mark.

In fact, both Cambridge and Oxford were named and defined and shown on their city arms as the merely prosaic river crossings, which their names still describe in modern English.

The *Domesday Book*, by which the Norman conquerors sought to make an inventory of their new lands, called this place Grantebrige, the name being simplified to Cambridge shortly afterwards.

Indeed, just as pedants in Oxford insist on the Thames within that city being called the Isis, so you will find the Cam here still called the Granta by many.

And this is not to say the Romans did not visit Cambridge at all. There are extensive remains at *Chester*ton in the north of the modern city. There was some kind of settlement on Castle Hill, probably called *Durolipons* (fortified bridge). It was very much on the edge of the patch administered from *Verulamium* (St Albans). But Cambridge was never a great city, or any city, of the Roman Empire.

One interesting thing is that we tend to think of the draining of the fens, the construction of canals to replace them and access by boats as something that happened in the last 400 years. If you know Cambridgeshire, you think differently. The Romans cut dykes and lodes to divert rivers and drain areas. These can still be seen 2,000 years later.

DANISH PASTING

The Dark Ages and early medieval period sees Cambridge enduring a stormy, frontier town history.

The marauding Danes – for whom the rivers were highways, not obstacles – burnt it in 871, occupied it in 875 and the small settlement that was Cambridge became part of Denmark in 878 by treaty. The Danes settled in the area now called Quayside.

The wars didn't stop, however, and the town was occupied by the Saxons who swore allegiance to the English king in 921. But Cambridge was attacked and burnt by the Danes one last time in 1010.

A few years later we have the *Domesday Book* snapshot of 'Grantebrige' with it paying geld to the king for a hundred hydes (a field size) of land.

The famed resistance fighter to the Norman invaders, Hereward the Wake, made the flooded fens his retreat from the conquering French-speakers. I say speakers because the Normans were really, as their name suggests, Norsemen in disguise.

The Normans built a castle in Cambridge, as they did all around England (such as the Tower of London), to cement their power over the resentful Saxons. Despite this, Cambridge was attacked during Norman succession struggles in 1088.

Cambridge, population of fewer than 2,000 souls, was still nowhere special. At some point in the Middle Ages the new route to London developed on the east bank of the Cam, that is the Trinity Street/King's Parade/Trumpington Road route still there today. Cambridge's prosperity grew because the bridge was the last crossing going down-river, and the market town could trade with the Continent as a port.

A SICK WIFE AND THE INFANCY OF ACADEMIA

The late 11th century sees some hints at what Cambridge would become, in the form of religious orders setting up here. They were, of course, commonplace throughout Europe and were powerful institutions. Learning to write was inseparable from religious learning – hence our words *clerk* and *clergy* are alike, although today they have totally different meanings. Cambridge (and Oxford) would not disentangle the Church from academic life until some eight or nine centuries later.

The Norman Sheriff of Cambridge, Picot, was a hated, ruthless man representing the Norman occupiers' wish to crush Saxon resistance. He was no friend to the Church. But he was so delighted by the 'miracle' of his deeply sick wife Hugolin's unexpected recovery in 1092 that he endowed an Augustinian order of monks to settle in Cambridge.

This, not the arrival of Oxford students more than a century later, may have been the first spark that gradually let the embers of academic thought glow and led, through centuries of fanning, to the blazing furnace of genius at Cambridge that was, one day, to dazzle all around.

The Augustinians are recorded as moving to Barnwell, off the Newmarket Road, in 1112 after Picot's son was accused of plotting and exiled. The land at Barnwell was given to one **Pain Peveril**, and there is still a chapel of the old Leper Hospital there today.

The name Barnwell denotes children's (possibly as in the Scottish *bairn*) spring. There is in Dugdale's *Monasticon Anglicanum* (1692) this explanation:

> Perceiving that the site on which their house stood was not sufficiently large for all the buildings needful to his canons, and was devoid of any spring of fresh water, Pain Peveril besought King Henry to give him a certain site near Cambridge ... from the midst of that site there bubbled forth springs of clear fresh water, called at that time in English Barnewell, the Children's Springs, because once a year on St John Baptist's Eve, boys and lads met there, and amused themselves in the English fashion with wrestling matches and other games and applauded each other in singing songs and playing musical instruments. Hence, by reason of the crowd that met and played there, a habit grew up that on the same day a crowd of buyers and sellers should meet in the same place to do business.

The Saxon jollifications at Barnwell moved a few hundred yards downstream – you would need good water for people and horses after all – and became known as the Starbridge or Stourbridge Fair which turned into a horse fair (the car auctions of their day), lasting until 1933. At one point it was said to be the biggest fair in Europe. And then in the 1960s a modern version of the fair was revived, so Pain Peveril's action still has effects 900 years later. A gipsy encampment associated with this fair was not moved away for the area to be developed until 1969, only some 857 years after the monks' move to Barnwell.

THE DEFILED VIRGIN AND PATRON SAINT OF LAUNDRY

Back to the gestation and infancy of what would become colleges. A Benedictine nunnery arrived a couple of decades later than the Augustinians and their nunnery of St Rhadegund was where Jesus College now stands.

Yet again the monastic order chose a site already made sacred by medieval well worship. There is still the sacred well of **St Rhadegund** sealed beneath the St Radegund pub in King Street across the road from the early nunnery. (St Rhadegund, by the way, was a pagan Thuringian princess who in 531 was defiled, aged 12, by the murderous King of Neustria. She married him but, failing to make him a better man, became a Christian with much washing and miracles – restoration of virginity being a particularly useful one. She became the patron saint of laundry, of all things).

These watery connections lead us to another root of the university in medieval Cambridge: the churches. St Bene't's (an abbreviation of St Benedict's), the oldest church, whose tower you still see today near King's College, stood here before any Normans did. Again it has an ancient well next to the steps into the churchyard, nowadays marked by a parish pump. Whether or not a few centuries earlier the new Christian religion took the sites of the holy wells, the churches in Cambridge were where teaching began.

The other large church, St Mary's-by-the-Market, was also used and it became Great St Mary's, the university church.

This is what led the students fleeing unrest in Oxford in 1209 (some of their fellows had been hanged merely for living in the same house as a murderer) to choose Cambridge. It was already a seat of learning, and was drawing the itinerant scholars and teachers off the roads to settle here. This date, however, is the first recorded in the history of the university – and the start of Cambridge's problems.

TOWN VERSUS GOWN: THE EARLY DAYS OF THE UNIVERSITY

Town versus Gown today seems light-hearted class rivalry between Toby and Araminta, on the one hand, and Dwane and Kylie on the other – except that as Cambridge becomes more and more an elite based on ability rather than background, such snob-versus-yob distinctions blur. But Town versus Gown goes

1246
Chancellor's Court set up

back to the infancy of the university and mirrored wider and deeper resentments that were to tear Cambridge, and eventually the nation, apart.

One of the earliest references to the existence of Cambridge University is in 1246, which mentions the Chancellor's Court.

Clearly, there must have been some kind of university to be chancellor of.

But this hints at the beginnings of an issue that was indeed to rip city, and later country, asunder: the fact that not all people were equal before the law.

The Chancellor's Court was where students and dons alike could insist on being tried for crimes of even great magnitude. This, the privilege of the Gown looking after its own, was to be for centuries a thorn in the side of the Town. Imagine – hundreds of lusty, young, bawdy, head-breaking, boozing students, armed with the daggers and bows and arrows which people carried in those days, and immune from punishment except by their own biased, protective legal system. If a townsman stole a sheep, he would be hanged. If a student did, he would almost certainly face a lesser penalty.

No wonder the Chancellor's Court became known locally as the 'Townsmen's Scourge'. The townsmen had no fair rights of redress against students breaking up the ale-houses, inns and shops, for example. This issue stirred up an anger which built up to an explosion, but not for a few centuries yet.

Meanwhile King Henry III had supported Cambridge University and granted its **first charter** (since lost), having invited students from the University of Paris to come here

9

after disturbances in France in 1229. In 1231 he had intervened in Town versus Gown disputes, ordering that lodging-house rents, which students were complaining about, be supervised by two masters and two honest townsmen called Taxors. This patched-up system survived for six centuries, until 1856.

TWO NATIONS UNITED – BY A COMMON DISLIKE

North versus South battles were another huge problem. As at Oxford and Paris, the nascent university was divided into *nations* according the scholars' origins. Here it was just two: Northerners, including any Scots (*Boreales*, as in the aurora over the pole), and southerners (*Australes*), coming from south of the Trent. Including Wales. So southerners were all Australians, by the standards of the day.

North v South? Today it is mere friendly rivalry, and one can imagine a *Carry On* film with flat-capped Northerners throwing black puddings and Yorkshire puds, or setting mooshy pea traps, while the smock-wearing Southerners retaliate with salvos of Cornish pasties and Melton Mowbray pork pies (they *would* be deadly, wouldn't they?).

One culture isn't right and the other wrong, just slightly different. The place names give away deep racial divides going way back to Angles and Vikings. Would a Southerner call a place Arkengarthdale, or a Northerner call one Nether Wallop? Never!

But while this all seems rather comical today, if you put, instead of Northerners and Southerners, Ulster Catholics and Protestants, or Palestinians and Israelis, the tone darkens to something closer to what it must have been. **Cambridge riots** between the nations were as bad as Town-and-Gown ones for causing death and destruction, and the two battles could merge into an unholy alliance of suspicious tribalism.

For instance, in 1261 the *Australes* and the Townies joined forces to attack the *Boreales*, a number of whom were killed and injured, and much property destroyed.

Some 16 Townies and 28 *Australes* were found guilty by the courts, yet the king told the judges to avoid hanging and mutilating the clerks (students), but to leave their chastisement to the university. Thus all 16 townsmen were punished and all 28 *Australes* pardoned, which again gives some measure of the unfair position of the Town versus Gown.

As for the Northerners, the *Boreales* were so angry, they tried to split the infant universities of Oxford and Cambridge into three, with many migrating in 1262 between the two, to Northampton, and starting one there. After all, hadn't many students migrated to Cambridge just half a century before because of being badly treated? Couldn't they leave the would-be university here to rot and do better on their own?

Many disgruntled Northerners ('chuffing 'eck, ah'm reet mithered, they're nobbut trooble') from both Oxford and Cambridge gathered at Northampton. In the event, history took a different turn and the king became concerned at Northampton's disrespect for his authority as part of a separate war with the barons. The embryonic university there was suppressed in 1265, the dreams of a northerners' Oxbridge stillborn, and Northampton became the abode of shoemakers instead. Cobblers, by 'eck, lad.

THE STINKING DITCH DEFENCE

In 1268 the islanders of Ely were being troublesome yet again and King Henry III ordered Cambridge to dig the defensive **King's Ditch** to form a moat, and erect gates at each end of the town (the Trumpington and Barnwell gates). As soon as the king and his army were gone, the Ely troublemakers burnt down the gates, pillaged a few homes and burnt them as well. The King's Ditch, far from being defensive, became rather offensive. It was piled with rubbish and excrement for hundreds of years, the pollution, disease and stink causing friction between Town and Gown, with complaints to Parliament and the king (until it was finally cleared out in 1610 by directing water from Shelford through it).

Medieval Cambridge was still small, around the two roads: Bridge Street going northeast/southwest and the other branching off this near the bridge and heading south. This road was then called the High Street (now St John's Street and Trinity Street, leading to King's Parade, and Trumpington Street) and led south to Trumpington Gate. This precious patch is still the heart of Cambridge; then it was *all* of Cambridge, jammed between the muddy river and a stinking ditch.

A PUKKAH UNIVERSITY – JUST IN TIME FOR THE BLACK DEATH

Meanwhile, in 1318, Pope John XXII issued the **papal bull** to declare Cambridge officially a pukkah university, a *studium generale*, with its own masters and scholars, free of the authority of the Bishop of Ely. This left the university to govern not only itself but also the town in many respects.

Meanwhile academia was soon booming with colleges being founded right, left and centre: Michaelhouse 1324, Clare Hall 1326, Pembroke Hall 1347, Gonville Hall 1348, Trinity Hall 1350, Corpus Christi 1352, King's Hall 1337ish. In 1343 the university gained rights to trial and punishment.

This collecting of more and more scholars and masters, all in one overcrowded place, was, sadly, just in time for the **Black Death**, which swept across England in 1348. It killed many – including 16 out of 40 scholars at King's Hall. It didn't help that people believed it was carried by dogs and cats, which were slaughtered wholesale, whereas we now know it was the fleas of rats which carried the plague. The misunderstood cats and dogs were the people's last defence, in fact.

The plague lingered on with many other illnesses now understood and largely conquered – for example, the ague, which may often have meant malaria. It was thought to be caused by bad air – hence *mal airia* – coming off stagnant pools and fetid ditches, of which there were certainly plenty around medieval Cambridge. In fact, it was, of course, the mosquitoes breeding in these ditches and carrying the parasite that killed young and old alike.

Even more annoying to the Town than the mosquitoes were the new wider powers of the Gown to interfere. The university licensed the ale houses, measured the bread and coal, weighed the grain, checked the butter, ran the market, forbade certain entertainments, opened the annual fairs and cracked down on loose women, houses of sin and evil persons. These latter categories are perhaps open to interpretation on flimsy evidence by the morals of the day, and, with the university proctors having the right to break down doors to check on the morals on those inside, one can sympathise with the Town.

When the Town's mayor went to the university authorities with complaints about scholars, he would be beaten up, have his robes torn, and be verbally abused. **Town v Gown** riots were therefore commonplace, with both sides distrusting the other, and many a head cracked.

The long-running riots (not to be sorted out until the mid 19th century) reached a high point in 1381, inspired to some extent by the **Peasants' Revolt** in the countryside. The Town attacked the Gown, burning all the charters and documents giving the hated university such power over them, and terrorised the scholars. The university treasures were looted.

Sadly, much of the early history of the university was destroyed in this riot: the documents were burned at the market with an old lady shouting: 'Away with the learning of the clerks' as priceless parchment after priceless parchment was destroyed. They aimed to kill the Bedell, a hated officer of the university, but he was wisely not at home when the mob arrived, so they wrecked his house instead. The town crier declared that the townspeople were entitled to kill the Bedell on sight.

Out in the nearby towns and villages the 1381 Peasants' Revolt – a sort of mass poll tax riot combined with general score settling – was put down with less violence than in other parts of the country, as it had been less severe in Cambridgeshire, although still widespread.

The Bishop of Norwich, who turned out to be a rather good soldier, led a force to crush the rebellion and swiftly restored order by beheading only one man in Cambridge's marketplace and hanging another. The good bishop went on to lead an army across East Anglia, slaying more and more of the rebels, even killing them at altars in the churches and monasteries they were caught sacking, driving them out of Norwich and eventually personally leading a cavalry charge against their last fortress. (I'd quite like to see a modern bishop giving it a go, in full regalia.)

In 1381 the university gained power over weights and measures in the whole town.

A great fire in Cambridge's tightly packed wooden buildings in 1385 did much to rid the town of the rats, plague and disease that thrived there.

1492
Gown powers increased over Town

In 1492 the Gown's powers increased yet again over the Town: the university gained the power of discommoning townsmen, that is banning them from supplying the university with commons – foodstuffs, etc.

THE FLAMES OF REFORMATION

We are entering the era where Cambridge would be known as 'Little Germany' for being a hotbed of Protestantism, where the Bible would scandalously be translated into English, and not restricted to Latin.

As stated above, the clerks of the university enjoyed 'benefit of the clergy' – that is, they could not be tried by public courts. The bitterness caused by such privileges – monks and nuns in those days were quite capable of embezzlement, theft, rape and prostitution – was one of the driving forces behind the Reformation which was to burst into a blaze in early 16th-century Cambridge.

Some historians, perhaps mindful of our present Royal Family's marital difficulties, say glibly that the **Reformation** was caused by Henry VIII's need for divorce. Only in so far as a wave is caused by a surfer. The tsunami of anger against the terminally corrupt Church – you could buy indulgences by paying a priest to receive forgiveness of even the most heinous crime, for example – was tearing across northern Europe. Many people wanted a return to the simple unadorned Christianity of the Church's beginnings, and Henry VIII was canny enough to ride this Protestant wave. But the

English monarch could not have withstood the surge of religious fervour for long. And Henry, having inherited a little of his father's financial sense, could see the vast lands and riches of the monasteries just waiting to be grabbed by him and his supporters.

Apologies for going over this bit of history that will be familiar to so many readers, but there are a couple of key Cambridge connections. Henry wanted to dump his wife Catherine of Aragon (so he could get hitched to Anne Boleyn) and couldn't get the Pope to annul his marriage, divorce not being a normal option then. He desperately cast about and one man, an obscure Cambridge cleric called **Thomas Cranmer,** came up with a formula that gave him a way to ditch Catherine (see page 83). It was enough to mark Cranmer out for greatness as Archbishop of Canterbury, and for martyrdom in the flames at Oxford when the Catholics took control once more.

The other Cambridge connection is the wooden screen at **King's Chapel** (page 191). The fact that this has Henry and Queen Anne Boleyn's initials entwined on it proves it was built in the 1,000 days between Anne becoming his queen and having her head chopped off. But why was he so driven to rip up the Church? Well, Anne refused to sleep with him until they were wed. A whole nation gets turned upside down because one lady 'plays hard to get'. Certainly worked on Henry.

Cambridge, more associated with Protestant radicalism than Oxford, was not without casualties in defence of the pope and Catholicism, even at the very top of the university.

One such martyr was Chancellor of the University **John Fisher** (1469–1535, and now a saint). He had a long, close association with the Tudor kings, having been confessor to Henry VII's mother Margaret Beaufort. Then he was Bishop of Rochester from 1504 to 1534. He had already become vice-chancellor of Cambridge University and later became chancellor. He helped Margaret Beaufort with her plans to set up St John's and Christ's Colleges and even became confessor to the afore-mentioned Catherine of Aragon, Henry VIII's first wife (the king being grandson to the Margaret whom Fisher had known so well).

He was vehemently against the corruption of the clergy which Protestants protested about, and was open to new learning such as that of Cambridge student Erasmus, but he did *not* want to destroy the one Church or tolerate heresies, as he would see it, such as Martin Luther's teaching. He stood out – the only bishop to do so – against the marriage of Henry VIII and Catherine of Aragon being dissolved, and the declaration that their daughter (Mary, later 'Bloody' Mary I who would wreak such revenge on behalf of Roman Catholics) was illegitimate. He refused to agree to the laws making Henry VIII supreme governor of the Church instead of the pope (and if this doesn't seem relevant history to today, then why are people asking how on earth Prince Charles can be titular head of the Church with his personal history of divorce and adultery?).

The result of his opposition to Henry VIII's policy was that John Fisher was defrocked in 1534 and thrown in the Tower of London. The pope in Rome, far from agreeing to his being defrocked, promoted him to cardinal in 1535. This so infuriated the king that he speeded up Fisher's trial and he was beheaded at the Tower in 1535 (a couple of weeks before the similar martyr Thomas More, as recreated in *A Man For All Seasons*, met the same fate).

The odd thing about the Reformation and Counter-Reformation in England, violent bloody battles as well as theological ones, is that though they started largely in Cambridge, it was Oxford where the better-known oppression and martyr burning took place. I quote from the twin to this book, *Eccentric Oxford*, because it's a powerful story that involves Cranmer, Latimer, also a Cambridge man, and Ridley:

Although the Reformation started more in Cambridge, by the middle of the 16th century Oxford was strongly Protestant. But by 1555 the Catholic Queen 'Bloody' Mary was the monarch. She ruthlessly tried to stamp out the new religion, and radical preacher (I was going to say firebrand but that would be too close to what comes next) Hugh Latimer and Prayerbook writers Nicholas Ridley and Thomas Cranmer were arrested and tortured near to death. Ridley and Latimer, who would not break their faith, were burnt at the stake in Broad Street – the cross in the roadway marks the terrible spot.

Dr Ridley's brother brought him a bag and tied it around his neck. Dr Ridley asked what it was and was told it was gunpowder. He said: 'I will take it to be sent of God and will receive it' and asked for some for his brother, meaning Latimer.

Then they brought a burning branch and put it in the heap at Dr Ridley's feet. Dr Latimer said: 'Be of good courage, Master Ridley, and play the man. We shall this day light a candle, by God's grace, in England that I trust will never be put out.'

19

Cranmer chickened out by signing a recantation. A year later, ashamed of himself, he dramatically recanted that recantation in St Mary's church and was also burned, famously thrusting his right hand into the flames to burn first as it had sinned by signing the confession the authorities wanted. Cost of burning the bishops: 11 shillings and fourpence (57p) for good dry firewood and labour.

PROGRESS AND PURITANISM

The restoration of a moderate form of Protestantism under Queen Elizabeth seemed to promise an end of the upheavals and extremism. She skilfully trod a middle way between the intolerant Puritan zealots and the Catholic-leaning right-wing, and although some outspoken Catholics got it in the neck – literally – her policy seemed to work, with Cambridge joining in the Elizabethan golden age of learning, the arts and the theatre.

But the seeds of the next century's conflict were being planted. In 1584 the puritan Sir Walter Mildmay founded **Emmanuel College**. The Queen met him at court and said: 'I hear, Sir Walter, that you have erected a Puritan foundation.' He replied – not without courage, as many a courtier including a better known Sir Walter Raleigh lost their heads: 'No, Madam. Far be it from me to countenance anything contrary to your established laws, but I have set an acorn which, when it becomes on oak, God alone knows will be the fruit thereof.'

The Roman Catholic threat to England was real, although it is fashionable to talk about them as mere victims nowadays, blamed for imagined plots. The blood-letting of Bloody Mary was, after all, nearly followed by the entire Houses of Parliament being blown to pieces in 1605, the thwarting of which Brits still celebrate with fireworks on 5 November. It would have been England's 5/11, in terms of terrorism.

But the Puritan threat on the Left was also real, and that Cambridge acorn planted by Sir Walter was soon growing well. The college was producing fundamentalist zealots by the score, and it is relevant that they were barred from staying there as fellows. Their mission was to infiltrate and undermine, to bide their time for the day when their views would be imposed as intolerantly as the Catholics'. Perhaps, with hindsight, Elizabeth should have chopped off this Sir Walter's head too and hacked down that sapling oak. Its powerful roots and grasping branches would in the not-too-distant future bring down the monarchy …

1561
Charter strengthens University's privileges

THE SCHOLARS AND THE PROCTORS: DISCIPLINE

One of the remarkable things about reading of former Cambridge students is how young they were. Ten, 12 years old on arrival was not unusual in the 16th and 17th centuries. Discipline was maintained by the university's own 'police' – the **proctors**, who rode about on white horses followed by their constables mounted on black.

These officials were supposed to wade into North v South, Town v Gown, Hostel v Hostel or College v College affrays, if not full-scale riots, right up until the 20th century.

The proctors, just to make their jobs harder, had no jurisdiction within colleges. This led to some curious situations such as the time a student was caught trying to climb out of a college window and stuck there. This was not in itself an offence, but not wearing a gown in the street was. Since the proctors could not apply the usual fine of 6s 8d (a third of a pound in old money) his top half only was fined, making it 3s 4d. The college could punish his bottom half.

CIVIL WAR, GREED, SLOTH AND DECADENCE

'Oh, did you guys have a civil war too?' queried the tourist outside Sidney Sussex, the audible 'R' of 'war' suggesting she was from that country that had its civil war later on, in the 19th century.

Yes, ma'am, we sure did, but you are forgiven for forgetting. It was, after all, in the 1640s and 1650s, 200 years before the United States one, and different in that it was a revolution too. An upheaval of the known order of things – with the king's head being one of many cut off – starting with the inefficient, corrupt, unfair, overtaxing, lazy governing classes getting a well-deserved kick up the jacksie. Then, just as in the French, Russian or Maoist revolutions, the combination of the shattering of the establishment with bigoted, vengeful, political or religious extremism soon led to new oppression, cultural vandalism and a new tyrant who made people think the *ancien regime* wasn't so bad.

In Cambridge's case the settling of old scores was another round in the 700 years' war between Town and Gown. Some of the colleges made the mistake of answering the king's call for financial assistance and suffered grievously for it when the Parliamentary army, with its intolerant Puritan ethic, gained the upper hand. The university was nearly destroyed, and the Town didn't mind the humbling of the dons.

And in Cambridge, the new national tyrant was one of their own – formerly an uncouth, loutish boy of 17 from nearby Huntingdon who had attended Sidney Sussex College – one Oliver Cromwell. Uncouth he may have been – his undergraduate years, he confessed later, had seen him a 'chief among sinners' – but as a soldier-statesman he was unrivalled, effective and ruthless, as his opponents in Scotland, Ireland and indeed Cambridge were to find out.

Again Cambridge's importance as a river crossing came to the fore, not now fearing invasion from the fens, but from the royal army down the Huntingdon road. The town had to be fortified and garrisoned. Cromwell, one of the town's MPs, ordered all the bridges destroyed except one.

Cambridge has on the whole been Left and radical compared to Oxford's Right and conservative, so it is hardly surprising that the king garrisoned the latter and the Parliamentary army the former. In the event Oxford saw battles and a siege whereas Cambridge, being somewhat out of the way then as now, did not.

After the **Restoration of the Monarchy** in 1660, Cambridge resumed its intellectual progress, with the arrival of one Isaac Newton being a damn good start.

The 18th century, on the other hand, was an era, in parts of Cambridge, of corruption, greed, sloth, decay and excess – to generalise. True, a lot of new professorships – in Arabic, botany, astronomy and modern history for example – were set up. The Senate House was built and written unseen examinations introduced. But many colleges saw standards of decay and drunkenness increase.

Other things did become better: the roads improved for the first time since the Romans, with Trumpington Road to London even having milestones installed, and turnpikes speeding up coach travel across the nation. In 1750 a timetabled coach service to London started. The bridges over the river were rebuilt and Addenbrooke's Hospital opened.

1744
The Cambridge Journal and Weekly Flying Post founded

A GROWING TOWN AND THE COMING OF THE RAILWAYS

The 19th century started with Enclosure Acts which let the town spread south and east. The creeping population growth of the previous dozen centuries was at last speeding up. In 1801 there were 9,276 inhabitants of the Town (not Gown); ten years later this had risen by 1,018, another ten years added 2,852, another ten brought 6,765, making the total 20,917 in 1831, thus doubled in size in just 30 years. Much more was to come.

In 1823 Magdalene Bridge was rebuilt (again), this time in iron.

Cambridge was still, however, a small town, untouched by the Industrial Revolution which transformed so much of Britain in the mid 19th century, when the Railway Age finally arrived here. It had been suggested that what became the east coast main line should go from London to Edinburgh through Cambridge, but a more direct route prevailed, and Cambridge had slumbered on undisturbed with its archaic stagecoach service.

In 1842 it was decided that Cambridge would after all be connected by railway with London, Peterborough and Suffolk. The powers-that-be at the university were horrified on three counts:

- Foreigners and the uneducated would come to Cambridge;
- Trains would run on the Sabbath, bringing ungodly noise and traffic to the town;
- Students might be tempted to use the routes and gain access to evil, sinful places they should not go to such as racecourses, fairgrounds, theatres or brothels.

(Right on all three counts, old chums, one is tempted to say now.)

The vice chancellor then argued that the railway plans were 'as distasteful to the university authorities as they must be to Almighty God and all right-minded Christians'. (I hadn't thought of God as a hater of the 08.15 to Liverpool Street, but then if you've tried it on a busy weekday, you may well think it a creation of the fellow with horns.)

In the event, Parliament, not the Almighty, took the decision to build the railway but the university insisted that the station be well away from the town, which has since condemned thousands of weary travellers to a good hike down Hills Road. It had the Act of Parliament say that not only would the Eastern Counties Railway not convey students, but it would be fined the then huge amount of £5 if it ever did so. The university officers were granted the freedom to inspect the platforms and trains at all times. And no trains were to arrive during the day on Sundays.

The 1867 station building was in a particularly pleasant arcade style and survives today. The original normal arrangement of two parallel platforms gave way to the odd single continuous platform with points halfway down so that two trains could be accommodated on it at once, like a waterfront with ships tied up. Hence it is one of the longest platforms in the country.

Meanwhile Cambridge's **Charles Darwin** completely overturns humanity's concept of history, creation (and thus scriptures to some extent) and science with his theory of evolution, initially outrageous, but now of global influence.

A law of 1856 ended the 700-year war between **Town and Gown**, with the university giving up its massive interfering powers. This didn't stop minor Town v Gown troubles at street level continuing up to the present day, with 'grad-bashing' a late-20th-century pastime. But the official conflict was over.

1856

Gown stops bossing around Town

In 1860, the university fellows were permitted to take a wife (their own, not anyone else's). Many Cambridge traditions, such as the May Balls, the Bumps races and the Oxford and Cambridge Boat Race, started in this century.

Massive reforms meant that Roman Catholics, Jews, Non-Conformists and eventually, yes, even women could attend the university. Girton and then Newnham Colleges were set up for women, but in 1897 the Senate in a stormy debate voted against awarding degrees to women (who could study to the same standard as men).

FROM THE FLIMSY FIRST AIRCRAFT TO SILICON FEN

The 20th century, besides the wars which took such a heavy toll of Cambridge men, saw many startling changes. Technology was moving on from the start. In 1910 moving pictures were shown in a marquee at Midsummer Fair, causing a sensation. A Blériot aircraft landed on Parker's Piece in 1911, to the astonishment of the populace. In 1919, with the end of World War I, the PhD was introduced to attract the brightest of foreign researchers. The 1930s saw the Guildhall and the University Library built.

Meanwhile Cambridge, always radical, produced a certain kind of Lefty – useful idiots Stalin called them – who thought betraying their country was the right thing to do out of idealism, with a rash of Cambridge-educated spies. And another great burst of Cambridge-centred literature.

World War II saw a mere 15 bombs and one crashing bomber hit Cambridge, which thus survived with its wonderful architecture intact, as did Oxford, leading some to suspect that Hitler thought he had some use for them. Again, many Cambridge men died in the conflict. In 1944 students and the American servicemen who flooded East Anglia during the latter part of the war had a drunken semi-riot and, unaware of Hitler's orders to the contrary, had a damn good go at wrecking the place.

The late forties brought proper degrees for women at long last.

The 1960s brought Churchill College and the new Addenbrooke's Hospital. The Rolling Stones came to town, as did Mini cars and miniskirts, and the first Cambridge Folk Festival. The Pill, rock 'n' roll, legalisation of homosexuality, the ending of book and play censorship and of the requirement of wearing gowns after dark all made their mark in Cambridge.

The 1970s brought loon trousers, organic food, Robinson College, Stephen Hawking and the first Cambridge Beer Festival. By the 1980s all colleges admitted women (and let them out again). But not all admitted men.

The Millennium brought the octocentenary of the Town Charter in January 2001. Perhaps octogenarian octuplets and octoroons should have eaten octagonal octopi in October to the sound of an octet playing octaves from an octavo, but a more conventional menu applied.

By the beginning of the 21st century, Cambridge's booming high-tech sciences and links with industries drawn to this hotbed of innovation had earned itself the nickname the **Silicon Fen** and a lot of breathless hype about 'the e-volcano at the end of the M11 that's about to erupt'. On the Science Park, in internet industries under the flight path of that flimsy canvas plane just a century before, they considered you had failed if you hadn't retired rich by the age of 34, the gushing hype told us.

Yet, for all this change, the wonderful small city that is Cambridge, a medieval marvel, compact county town and intellectually invigorating as always, retains its charm, its hidden passages and its surprising green spaces and beautiful vistas that continue to delight. The essence of Cambridge is that it always has one foot in the cloistered Middle Ages and the other striding way into the unimaginable and brilliant future. Amazing discoveries that shattered mankind's understanding and overturned everything we thought we understood were made repeatedly at Cambridge – laws of motion, evolution, discovery of the electron, splitting the atom, DNA, as well as towering works of literature and art – and there will be more from Cambridge. The thousand-year story of this intense little town with an astounding impact on the world ain't over yet.

1953

DNA discovered

2 Eccentric Legends

Three great Cambridge heroes and zeroes

THE CHARIOTS OF FIRE AND THE FOUR-MINUTE MILE

If you are very, very old you might remember the startling triumph against the odds at the 1924 Paris Olympics of two very different British runners, **Harold Abrahams**, a Jewish Cambridge man, and Eric Liddell, a Presbyterian Scot who famously refused to run on the Sabbath.

If you are pretty old, you'll recall the way civilian Westerners in the Far East were interned in often barbaric circumstances in World War II, a story recalled in the book and film *Empire of the Sun*.

If you are merely quite old, you might – no you will – recall the first four-minute mile, run at Oxford in 1954, which was as much a sensation as climbing Everest had been the previous year.

If you are middle-aged or younger you might well remember the film *Chariots of Fire* which brilliantly recreated the story of Abrahams and Liddell.

And if you are rather young, you might remember Trinity College, Cambridge, refusing to allow a re-run of the famous race around the Great Court, against the striking of the clock, which featured in that film.

All of these are connected, and Cambridge-connected, and make a great yarn which tells us a lot about changing attitudes over the past 100 years.

Harold Abrahams was the Caius College student who ran in the 1924 race. It was triumph over adversity because Jews were widely disliked at the time. This was before the Nazis had exposed anti-semitism and racism for the outright evil it really was; many snobby British people casually looked down on Jews and other races (although many more didn't). He had entered the 1920 Antwerp Olympics and done badly. He'd hired a coach, frowned on by some lovers of amateurism (this love of amateurism has its limits: see *Scott of the Antarctic*, page 176).

The Scot Eric Liddell was supposed to be a favourite for the 100 metres in 1924 but withdrew, as his religion demanded, when it was scheduled for the Sabbath. Abrahams, who naturally had no Sunday observance, took the gold his fellow Briton had hoped for.

Liddell was switched to the 400 metres, a distance he'd rarely run in and was expected to fail at, having trained for the very different short sprint. He won gold to the delight of Scotland, the rest of Britain and Christians everywhere, who took it as his reward for observing the Sabbath. In fact, he set a world record, which feat he attributed to God's help.

Liddell had been born in China, and wanted to become a missionary there, which he did. He was still there when the Japanese invaded – having sent his family to safety – and was put in an internment camp in 1943. He died there in 1945 as the war ended.

Rolling the calendar on another decade, we come to Roger Bannister's triumph in running the first four-minute mile (well, under four minutes, obviously, but only just). This took place at Oxford, but a little-known fact is that Harold Abrahams was a timekeeper at the running track on that day – 6 May 1954. It was sensational and made headlines around the world. Abrahams's reaction to the time being announced summed up the importance of the four-minute mile. 'When I heard the words "three minutes …", it was as if an atom bomb had gone off.' The rest of the time was lost in cheering.

An eccentricity featured in the film about the 1924 Olympics, *Chariots of Fire*, was the famous Trinity College, Cambridge, Great Court Run, in which students supposedly ran the 367m around this quad in the 43 seconds that the clock takes to strike twelve (at noon on the day of the matriculation dinner), the aim being to arrive back before the last stroke.

The film shows Abrahams, who after all was at Cambridge, winning such an annual race.

Not only is this completely untrue, but if you know Cambridge you will surely know that the quadrangle featured in the film is *not* that at Trinity. How did these myths grow up? Was such a race complete fiction?

Well, not entirely. Having asked this question in a national newspaper, it turned out that this feat was achieved at least once, by Lord Burghley in 1927 running against no-one except the chimes at midnight, not noon, and after a rather good dinner.

The great British Olympic runners of another generation ran a charity version of the Great Court Run in 1988. Sebastian Coe, who later became Lord Coe and masterminded the bringing of the 2012 Olympics to London, raced against Steve Cram. Coe beat the clock's usual 43-second time, but because the mechanism had just been wound by an over-helpful college porter, the clock struck faster than normal and beat him, so I consider he lost.

It turns out that the Great Court Run in the film was shot at Eton College, which has a suitable quad, because the fellows of Trinity feared being portrayed as anti-semitic in the movie, an attitude which, as I say, was then not so rare in the upper classes.

It fell to an aristocratic lady, writing to a newspaper in 2005, to put the record straight, and I reproduce her proud letter with permission:

> The film *Chariots of Fire*, while excellent in many ways, has given rise to a complete myth by portraying Harold Abrahams as winning an annual race against undergraduates. Not only did Abrahams never run round Trinity Great Court (it wasn't his distance), there was never a race between athletes. It was run only by my father, Lord Burghley, against the clock, probably after a dinner party, before returning to his own college. The family is proud of this achievement and dismayed that it has been misportrayed. My father also ran around the decks of the Queen Mary in two minutes, a feat recorded on a plaque on the ship herself. Luckily, the film makers seem not to have been aware of this. *Lady Angela Oswald, King's Lynn, Norfolk.*

RUPERT BROOKE: GOLDEN POET OF A GOLDEN AGE?

A subtitle for this section might be: 'Or foppish wally and pretentious prat who died most unheroically while inspiring others to feed the needless massacre of World War I?'

Rupert Chawner Brooke (1887–1915), the famed poet of the Great War who died early in that conflict, and who went up to King's from Rugby School in 1906, was the one man who made a certain Edwardian style of Britishness, more precisely Englishness, and particularly Cambridgeness, and yes, even Grantchesterishness, known right across the world. If anyone knows any two lines of poetry from that rather extraordinary era, then it is either the cloying, sentimental poem about Grantchester, the village outside Cambridge where he once lived (written in a Berlin café by the homesick young graduate in 1912):

Stands the Church clock at ten to three?
And is there honey still for tea?

Yes, OK, it is syrupy, a bit like the vacuous guff 1960s prime minister's wife Mary Wilson used to write or Patience Strong would pen for soppy women's magazines. But hang on a minute, if you read the whole thing, with its mocking satire of all the Cambridge villages in turn, you will see it is supposed to be entertainingly light and humorous, and nothing more.

Sorry, I said 'either' and didn't get to the 'or'. Or, that more serious poem 'The Soldier' starting:

If I should die, think only this of me:
That there's some corner of a foreign field
That is for ever England. There shall be
In that rich earth a richer dust concealed;

> A dust whom England bore, shaped, made aware,
> Gave, once, her flowers to love, her ways to roam,
> A body of England's, breathing England's air,
> Washed by the rivers, blest by suns of home.

A couple of lines, did I say? Sorry, but you can't stop with verses that are so confident, and Brooke hadn't forgotten (unlike many later poets) that rhyme means we can't forget either. Why quote just a couple of lines when the drum-like repetition of 'England' is what makes the verse work?

And Edwardian poets such as Brooke's contemporary, Oxford's Edward Thomas (killed in the same war) wrote poems anyone could understand on first reading, which is *not* to say Thomas or Brooke were shallow. Far from it.

A SHORT LIFE Brooke was in many ways a golden youth of a golden age, and dying at the height of your fame is always an excellent career move in fixing your fame in the affections of the public before you become tarnished, as Nelson and Shelley had shown before, and J F Kennedy and Jimi Hendrix would later.

So-called war poet Brooke never really reached the front line, some of his critics say, and died prosaically of a fly bite and blood poisoning on the way to Gallipoli, and has thus been attacked for his patriotic, verging on heroic-jingoistic view of the war, compared to those poets who did see the horrendous slaughter of the trenches.

Decades later, in the post-World War II rejection of Britishness, imperialism and militarism, his attitudes were cited as virtually the *cause* of the war. The idea that war would be noble, gallant, romantic, short and chivalrous, instead of drowning in gas and mud, mowed down by machine-guns in pointless attacks that could not possibly work in bungled campaigns – as the later poets depicted with gloomy, tragic realism – was unrealistic. The kind of feelings Brooke expressed at the start of the war had men flocking in their thousands for a glorious war famously expected to be over by Christmas.

All this is unfair, being wise after the event. It is hardly Brooke's fault that he died at the beginning. The other poets, who exposed the true horrors later, were at the time writing similar optimistic, patriotic and unrealistic stuff (Wilfred Owen in particular did a 180° turn in his attitudes when he saw what trench warfare actually meant).

And the poets like Thomas, who lived until near the end of the war, and even those driven mad by it and locked up in asylums, didn't reject those earlier, simple poems on the unspoiled Edwardian countryside – that vision is what kept them going. That England is what they were fighting for.

THE GOLDEN AGE: EDWARDIAN ENGLAND BEFORE THE STORM If you forget any idea of Rupert Brooke's being a war poet, or even a truly great poet, his short life and lasting poetry have an enduring beauty and an insight into the attitudes of what indeed seems in some ways a golden age, at least for the middle and upper classes. It was the Edwardian era, unaware of the volcanic eruption about to sweep all of it away, the last hurrah of a rigid class system that had many born to service, some to middle-class respectability and a few to aristocracy.

Britain was at the centre of the greatest empire history had ever seen, and a seemingly benign one run with the assent of most of the people involved (and no-one dreamed it would be gone in half a century).

British industry and technology was the best, the engineering, ships, railway engines and bridges the grandest, and the Royal Navy ruled the seas, having by and large kept global peace since 1815. The arts reflected this confidence (consider Elgar's music, Shaw's plays, etc) and people believed in science and civilisation and progress.

The English countryside described by Brooke, Thomas and others was still beautiful, still farmed by hand and horse, with little noise or chemical pollution, with villages that rarely saw outsiders and life continued as for centuries. If Edwardian Englishmen were too confident of the superiority of their civilisation – an attitude, when it became arrogance, that would hasten the rejection of the Empire around the world – then it was at least based on real achievement. The country was Number One, and knew it was the most successful in history.

It was perhaps like being American in 1962, before things started going wrong with assassinations, Vietnam, terrorism, the feeling that people hated you for reasons you didn't quite understand, and the realisation that the politicians in charge of your country weren't as morally pure and heroic as you once imagined.

Into this scene strode the near six-foot handsome young Brooke with his shock of reddish-gold hair, well versed in poetry by his Rugby School housemaster father.

The boy was a good actor and a hit on the sports field at both cricket and, naturally, rugby, the real man's sport born at that very school. My own grandmother, who met the schoolboy Brooke, endorsed the impression of a greatly gifted, golden young man. He was charming, witty. You noticed him in a crowd, a room fell silent when he walked in. If as the contemporary Kipling (or maybe Rhodes, no-one is sure) put it: 'To be born an Englishman is to have won first prize in the lottery of life.' It seems fate had also dealt Brooke personally a winning hand of cards.

One of the fascinating things about the *jeunesse dorée* of this summer, before the storms to come, is how connected they were. They all seemed to know each other, looking back. Brooke's friends at Cambridge included E M Forster, Virginia Stephen (Woolf to be), George Mallory (who was to die on Everest, possibly having conquered the peak), Keynes the economist, Hugh Dalton (who was to become a government minister, set up the Special Operations Executive in World War II and then became Chancellor of the Exchequer), and Frances Cornford (the poet, granddaughter of Charles Darwin who later married Professor Francis Cornford, which sounds more confusing than it was).

Cornford, the poet, wrote of the young Brooke:

A young Apollo, golden-haired,
Stands dreaming on the verge of strife,
Magnificently unprepared
For the long littleness of life.

Everyone Brooke met fell under his spell to some extent. In 1909 we find Brooke punting the novelist Henry James up the Cam to Grantchester (although he let the wet pole slip through his fingers and crash on to James's bald head). James, also dazzled by something about the youth, was told that Brooke was a poet, but not a very good one. He replied: 'Well I must say I am relieved, for with that appearance if he had also had talent it would be too unfair.'

Brooke joined the Royal Naval Division (despite its name a land force formed with the help of sailors from key ships). It isn't quite true that he never saw war at all, for he took part in the abortive expedition to Antwerp in October 1914 when he saw the refugees fleeing the German advance, atrocities and all, and the city burning.

In March 1915 his Hood Battalion embarked on a troopship for a secret destination in the Mediterranean. With his classical education, Brooke guessed where they were heading rather well, and wrote in a letter with enthusiasm for the coming conflict (which would be a drawn-out bloody failure, as it turned out):

> Do you think perhaps the fort on the Asiatic corner will want quelling, and we'll land and come at it from behind and they'll make a sortie and meet us on the plains of Troy?

Nothing there about being machine-gunned and slaughtered by the hundred while repeatedly charging barbed wire uphill in a terrible stalemate, or being humiliated by the Germans' allies the Turks.

On the way there via Egypt, he caught dysentery, heat stroke and then blood poisoning caused by a fly bite on his lip. He died on 23 April, St George's Day and Shakespeare's birthday. His name is carved on the wall of the memorial side chapel in the glorious King's College Chapel as if he too fell in battle, but his end was more prosaic.

This heroic Apollo, this would-be great warrior, brought down by a fly. He was buried on the Greek island of Skyros.

As with Hendrix's albums, Brooke's poetry books sold vastly more after his death than before.

Brooke's fame endured then because his poems stood as a symbol of patriotic heroism, and now for a slaughtered generation of wasted talent, a link with a golden age that the guns destroyed. And on Skyros, where there is a statue of Brooke and a square named after him, just as Brooke foresaw, there *is* still in a corner of a foreign field, a richer dust concealed, that is for ever England.

ONE MAN'S OBSESSIVE QUEST TO KILL AN EMPEROR

Among the pleasantly battiest of 20th-century Cambridge eccentrics was a superb specimen of that well-known breed of oddballs, British butterfly collectors: **Ian Robert Penicuick Heslop** (1904–70).

Of course, nowadays they tend to photograph the little blighters but in the early 20th century they caught them, killed them with poison and stuck them on display boards as specimens. Especially the rare ones. The more you got, the better, bizarrely – a little like collecting stamps (well, more difficult to catch, and less useful stuck on letters, but the obsession with finding that extra one could be similar).

Heslop, one of the extreme variants of the human species, was to throw himself in front of speeding railway trains when chasing a rare butterfly, or immerse himself in bogs fully clothed, or fall from trees reaching for a butterfly on the furthest branch.

Born in India, where his father was a soldier, Heslop grew up in Bristol. The decisive moment in his life came when, aged seven and in bed suffering from mumps, a kindly aunt gave him a couple of cabbage white larvae (caterpillars to you and me) in a jar to look after. These wriggly fellows duly became butterflies and the boy was hooked. Parental bans only encouraged him. He discovered that crushed laurel leaves were excellent for killing the captured creatures, and by 1921 he had captured the rare Camberwell beauty.

In 1923 he went up to Cambridge, where he read classics, became good at rifle shooting and collected butterflies. On graduating, he took a course in colonial administration and in 1928 became an administrator in Nigeria.

Heslop took a great interest in the flora and fauna, shooting a good deal of the latter and discovering a rare form of pygmy hippopotamus which he named after himself *Hexaprotodon liberiensis heslopi*. He wrote learned reports with unlikely sentences in them such as:

> I have recently discovered that the extremely rare Brown-chested Wattled Plover occurs sparingly near Okigwi during the dry season.

Someone's got to care about the little chaps, haven't they? And of the human population:

> The Nkalus are on the whole not likeable people. Their extraordinary deceitfulness and lack of good faith towards each other is their most repulsive characteristic.

('So on the whole you're not terribly keen on them then, Heslop, old chap?' you can imagine his superiors saying. And this crushing judgement certainly does not apply to any living Nkalus, particularly those with good lawyers.)

Having raised a family partly in Nigeria and partly in England – where he returned for his annual leave always in the purple emperor season (excited diary entry at Petworth, July 1935: 'This was my first capture of His Imperial Majesty, the Purple Emperor, monarch of all butterflies') – Heslop returned for good in 1952, and became a Latin teacher by profession, butterfly nut by character.

As his biographer, butterfly expert Matthew Oates – to whom I'm totally indebted for the information in this account – wrote: 'One might expect Heslop, after almost 25 years in Africa, away from the classics, to have forgotten every word he had ever learnt.' In fact, he had remembered everything, and naturally chose the various schools where he taught because they were within purple emperor territory (Wiltshire, Hampshire and West Sussex).

Heslop spotted his first wood white *Leptidea sinapsis* while waiting on a railway station. The butterfly settled on the track. Oates quotes him:

> I jumped down on to the track to the accompaniment of a shout from the railwayman: 'Look out, there's a train coming!' (and indeed I could feel in my face the draught forced from the tunnel) caught my first wood white and leapt back on the platform just as the train emerged from the tunnel a few yards away.

What the express train driver, whistling furiously at what seemed a total nutter, said is sadly not recorded.

Another time he crashed from a too-thin branch of an oak tree 20ft above the ground, but the black hairsteak he had captured was unharmed. After that he took to using an enormous 37ft-6in-long butterfly net, as tall as a house.

Heslop regarded rare butterflies, eccentrically, as big game, similar to the beasts he had shot in Africa. He said in 1953: 'By a coincidence I have caught as many purple emperors as I have shot elephants.'

It was at about this time that we find him experimenting with bait to draw the elusive emperors within range of his net and his 'lethal cup' killing jar. He had a trailer load of cow dung dumped in some woods in Wiltshire. Then he tried deer skins, a dead snake, rotting bananas, sugar, strawberries and beer. In the end he found it was leaking sap of a certain oak tree which the emperors just couldn't resist.

Even into his sixties we find his diary recording his amazing efforts to find a large copper at Woodwalton Fen, which he used to visit by motorbike in his Cambridge days. To get there he started at Salisbury station at 06.00, arrived at Huntingdon at 11.12 and took a taxi to the fen, which was heavily flooded. The warden was trying to rescue cattle but this, of course, did not put off Heslop. He waded up the main drove. 'I was soon waist deep and then up to my armpits; and one moment I went right under.'

But he plugged on to the secret spot where the large copper lurked (the butterfly, not the policeman), and bagged a fine series for his collection, walking, wading and swimming back in his sodden clothes in time to catch the 18.13 train home, reached after midnight. The diary entry ends: 'The station cat at Huntingdon is 21 years old.' He was 64 years old.

A year later we find his diary entry for the day man first walked on the moon, 21 July 1969. A historic day, evidently – he had caught an amazingly rare pristine male purple emperor aberration *iole* (not with white bands and spots, but you knew that, of course). So he wrote excitedly: 'Never have I taken an insect more easily! It was just flying peacefully along the track at knee height.'

A year later Heslop was as dead as the beautiful ranks of his butterfly collection, all pinned up and labelled with time and place of capture and still to be seen at Bristol City Museum (the butterflies, not him, although that would have been a fitting end).

3 Eccentric People

More of Cambridge's most fascinating eccentrics, living or dead

THE UNBELIEVABLE, THE HORRID AND THE HILARIOUS

SNOWY FARR Surely one of Cambridge's best-loved eccentrics of the late 20th and early 21st century, Snowy Farr was a striking sight in Cambridge with his scarlet uniform and broad-brimmed hat (see cover picture). He'd entertain visitors to the city by letting live mice run around the broad brim of his hat, and then by popping one into his mouth, which didn't seem to do the mouse a great deal of harm, while Snowy breathed through his nose (avoiding mouth-to-mouse respiration). Meanwhile a pigeon or cat would be perched on the top of the hat, which must have kept those mice moving all the faster.

Snowy Farr, a retired road sweeper from Oakington, did it all for charity and over the years raised well over £60,000 for local blind people. Back in 1977, Snowy had constructed a weird tricycle trailer thing carrying various animals including a kitten, a chicken and a duck in order to re-enact the Pied Piper story. In a way it worked, for 150 parents and their children had turned up willing to follow the bizarre procession, and others joined in.

The result was chaos as some cycling children went ahead and got lost, while a fire broke out at the Whim restaurant in Trinity Street and three blaring fire engines joined the fun. Some children went in one direction singing *Old MacDonald Had a*

Farm while others went the opposite way. Police were called to rejoin the two streams of happy children and parents while onlookers thought Cambridge had gone completely bonkers.

Snowy's unorthodox fundraising later received official recognition when he was invited to Buckingham Palace to collect an MBE medal, although less so from Cambridge Council in 1999 when he was ordered to remove the hundreds of flags and teddy bears that populated his front garden. As eccentric old Snowy's life was spent helping the visually handicapped, perhaps turning a blind eye would have been the thing.

RICHARD COLLINS He likes to cycle into Cambridge from Hardwick, about five miles west of the city, for a bit of shopping or to walk around the gardens of nearby stately homes such as Anglesey Abbey. Nothing eccentric about that. So do many people, but Richard sometimes does it naked. He was photographed pedalling along the Newmarket Road by the *Cambridge Evening News*. The lifelong naturist was quoted by them as saying: 'Nude cycling is, I've found, one of the best ways to combine exercise with enjoying the sun and air on my body. It's exhilarating and fun. I rarely get any adverse comments or reactions.' No-one seems that bothered. To break the law in this regard you have to deliberately expose certain parts *and* intend that someone will see them and be caused alarm and distress. When I say certain parts I don't mean ears, obviously, or Prince Charles and Andrew Marr would be in big trouble (both are Cambridge graduates, by the way).

Having caught up with Mr Collins, I found out how his interest in naturism started.

'When I was in my early twenties my girlfriend and I took our motorboat on holiday to Poole Harbour in Dorset. We headed out to sea and, thinking that Bournemouth beach would be overcrowded, headed for Studland beach. As I grappled with the anchor, and we got closer, I suddenly realised that everyone on the beach was naked! We'd arrived right in the middle of a naturist beach! I thought, when in Rome, so we stripped off too.

'I've always enjoyed sunbathing, and it seemed the "natural choice" to go for an all-over tan, so we discarded our cossies. It felt great and I've never looked back.

'I married my girlfriend and our children have grown up with naturism, but they've all grown out of it – as they do – except me!

'I sometimes go riding without clothes in the countryside. I love the feeling of freedom with the sun and air on my skin – while combining it with some exercise. One hot day I got to Coton village and thought: "Why put shorts on just to go though Cambridge?" and just carried on. I passed the cricket ground and they all cheered!

'On the whole people are positive, but I always carry something to "cover up" in case anyone gets upset. I used to carry a T-shirt draped over the handlebars but now, confident that I'm doing no harm and breaking no laws, my clothes go safely in a backpack.

'I usually wear a sarong when shopping in town, it's the easiest thing to don while sitting on a bike! Why the sarong? I guess I feel naked without my bike!'

CHARLIE CAVEY Bin there, done that. If you hear a litter bin apparently singing to you in Cambridge, don't worry. It's pavement performer Charlie Cavey, a music student at the other university in town, who squeezes into a round litter bin to belt out Tom Jones, Cat Stevens, Oasis and Elvis classics on his guitar for passers-by, only the neck of the guitar suggesting that the disembodied voice might belong to someone. It looks like

a proper, council-owned, cast metal bin, and is indeed marked 'litter', so you wonder what Charlie's done with the litter and whether people throw chip wrappers etc on his head. The answer is that although it is a proper bin, busker Charlie bought this one and drags his stage – possibly the world's smallest – with him. Or did do until it was stolen in 2006. At the time of writing he was saving up for a new litter bin to warble from. At least he won't be offended if passers-by react by saying: 'Rubbish!' Sorry, Charlie, that was a throwaway line … Meanwhile adaptations of Tom Jones hits could include: *It is Unusual; What's New, Litter Lout; I'll Never Fall in the Trash Again.*

KIM DE LA TASTE TICKELL It is fortunate, perhaps, that this deeply eccentric publican is dead, and yet personally I miss him. For if you visited the Tickell Arms, at

Whittlesford, near Cambridge, when he was in charge, you would assuredly have been insulted – that is what people in the know went there for. I recall going up there in the 1970s with a friend who drove some kind of Lotus wafer-thin mint car, the sort you insert yourself in like a legal document being put in a long envelope.

After occasionally touching the A505 while flying up from Baldock to Royston, my show-off chum parked the car with the usual flamboyant rev of the engine. This, of course, was the cue for the landlord. 'You can't park that f****** monstrosity there,' he bellowed across the lawn, setting the tone, and wearing some kind of 18th-century outfit involving knee breeches and an eye-glass on a ribbon round his neck. My chum moved his Lotus, scraping it on some sort of obstruction. 'Mind my rocks when you're parking,' said Tickell, much cheered up by the damage, 'they're bloody expensive,' before yelling at some passing unfortunate 'Get off my f****** grass!' We learned he had just thrown out a customer who had ordered the finest wines and food, because he had been rude to one of his waitresses *two years before.*

He banned lefties, anyone wearing a CND badge (that is ban the bomb, a big deal in the 1960s so it would have once included many students and dons, all of whom he described as 'destestable and disloyal to the Crown'), any racial minority he disapproved of, which was all of them, and 'modern women', whatever they were. He would keep a pair of large scissors handy to snip off any tie he disapproved of and once, sensing guests were not to his liking, screeched: 'I'm not having a bunch of south London garage proprietors and their tarts in here. Out, out, *out!*' If he was particularly annoyed he would seize one of the medieval weapons from the walls of the pub, such as a mace or halberd, and brandish it at the people he wanted to drive away. He ended up in court as a result at least once.

The food, I remember, was rather good, with things you don't normally eat: smoked pike was good if bony, and the pigeon was delicious apart from having to spit out lead shot. Kim de la Taste Tickell (his name was, oddly, as christened apart from the Kim part, being the local squire in effect) died in 1990, 'not a moment too soon' as a local said rather bluntly. He was, unsurprisingly, unmarried. The food is today even better, but now comes without large dollops of politically incorrect insults. Whether you prefer it that way is up to you.

THOMAS HOBSON You may have heard the expression 'Hobson's choice' – meaning no choice at all. This originated with Thomas Hobson (1544–1631), a carter on the London–Cambridge route of Shakespeare's day who has left a mark to this day on Cambridge's face and on the English language. As well as making a good living carting the trunks of students and belongings of academics, Hobson also had livery stables where St Catharine's College stands today, at which you could hire a horse, with a corresponding stable in the City of London. In order to use the horses efficiently (instead of working the best-looking ones into the ground), he did not allow customers to pick their horse, as at most stables of the era, but offered them in strict rotation. Thus Hobson's choice – the next one or nothing.

The mark he left on Cambridge's landscape is the hexagonal stone Hobson's Conduit, which you pass coming up the Trumpington Road into Cambridge from the southeast. It is hard to overestimate the importance of clean water to town dwellers in previous centuries when people died in their dozens from water-borne diseases such as cholera. Water had to be carried from safer, upstream places, but even then was a danger. Many people drank beer, even at breakfast time (I know a don who still does) and gave it to their children because the brewing process killed the bugs. Hence the warnings about the perils of drinking small beer, the weak stuff.

It was to deal with this bugbear of Cambridge Town and Gown that the carter Thomas Hobson provided a fancy conduit, now seen in exile on the Trumpington Road, but sited by him at Market Hill, near Petty Cury, for the convenience of townspeople. It stood there from 1614 to 1856 when it was moved after a fire in the market, piped water having made it less necessary. The water for the conduit came from springs and Hobson merely provided the outlet, others having started the project earlier. His name was on the outlet, so it was good for his PR sense – we're still talking about him today, and there's a Hobson Building and Hobson Street in the city. For more than two centuries townspeople would have remembered Hobson for the fresh spring water, which was piped under the road, flowing ceaselessly from the four spouts.

When Hobson died in 1631 he left some lands to pay for keeping his conduit perpetually in order. Even today the water brought into Cambridge still flows along the consequently named Brookside to Hobson's conduit. Much of it goes on down deep runnels either side of Trumpington Street, nicknamed the Pem and Pot, which seem like traps for motorists parking badly. I'm told the colleges still use Hobson's water for certain purposes (gardens, fountains, pools, hosing down people from Oxford, etc). It is possible for the city engineers to divert the water into conduits, so if the runnels are dry, it's running in tunnels. There were or are branches all over the place – to the basement of the hospital, to various college ponds, even to a one-time pond at Parker's Piece.

HENRY FAWCETT (mail role model) While a promising young undergraduate at Trinity Hall, Henry Fawcett (1833–84) went on a shooting party with his family. A blunder by his father, with his gun discharging in the wrong direction, cost Fawcett his sight, permanently, in an age when such a disability could mean poverty or at least dependence. Young Fawcett, however, felt his father's sadness so acutely that he tried all the harder to excel. He still took part in sport, fishing, rowing in eights, riding and once famously skating at high speed with friends on the frozen Cam from Ely to Cambridge. He hit a bad patch of ice but called to his friends: 'Go on, go on! I've only got my legs through.' On another occasion, a friend took him to Royston Heath so he could roam without danger on the soft grass. Fawcett loved 'climbing the mountains at Royston', as he imagined them, so much that he frequently returned.

Henry Fawcett became a professor of political economy and then an MP. His daughter became senior wrangler at Cambridge aged only 20; his wife Millicent (née Garrett) was a great campaigner for votes for women; and together the Fawcetts made plans for five young women to start being educated at Regent Street, Cambridge – a radical move that was to lead to the creation of Newnham College.

Meanwhile Fawcett became Postmaster General and reformed this whole institution with his usual energy and brilliance, inventing the parcel post and the word 'postman' instead of 'letter carrier', and advocating work for women at every level at a time when many people thought them not capable. When he died aged only 51 the procession of loyal postal staff from around the country, going behind the coffin to Trumpington Church where his grave may still be seen, was a mile long. The postmen's stamp of greatness.

SYD BARRETT (founder member of the Pink Floyd rock group; died 7 July 2006) Born in Cambridge in 1946 Roger Keith Barrett, usually known as Syd, became reclusive after hitting the big time with the 1960s psychedelic super group and bouncing off. He was dogged by ill health of various types, and rarely spoke to the media during the four decades he lived in Cambridge. But the way rock fans work, this has only increased their fascination with this genius for ever associated with the global hit, *Dark Side of the Moon*. However, this didn't stop a band called the Television Personalities putting out a track called *I Know Where Syd Barrett Lives* amid a remarkable number of musical tributes.

He was misnamed Syd as a teenage musician because, some say, a previous drummer in a band was called Syd and they couldn't be bothered to change the name (there was a time when all lawyers in Scotland seemed to be called Hugh, so I know what they mean). He moved to London in the mid-sixties to go to the trendy Camberwell Arts College and met old friend and musician Roger Waters. They formed a band, naming it after two Georgia blues artists Pink Anderson and Floyd Council (so if you were young thereabouts, you very nearly spent hours sitting around in darkened flats listening to Anderson Council). Syd became the songwriter. The band was very experimental with lights, electronics and any other substances that sprang to mind (don't say that Syd did anything illegal, a passing Hugh tells me). Syd became increasingly eccentric, refusing to perform on stage (although happy to practise) and refusing media interviews. One American tour was totally stuffed up in the process. Syd bust up with the band and recorded two solo albums, *The Madcap Laughs* and *Barrett*, and then retreated to Cambridge. He ventured down to the studio in London a few years later where the remainder of the Floyd were recording a sort of tribute to him, *Shine on You, Crazy Diamond*, but he had changed so much the band didn't recognise him. He soon tired of sleeping on people's floors in London and walked back to Cambridge.

AA MILNE For someone whose Winnie-the-Pooh books achieved staggering success, Trinity College graduate Alan Milne – known by millions worldwide as simply A A Milne – was surprisingly Eeyore-like about it all. He didn't want to be known for his books on the shelves of the children's section of bookshops and libraries, but for his 25 plays, poems and detective stories, which are now mostly forgotten. But then he didn't want his first job at *Punch* magazine, where he started work aged 24, and he certainly didn't want to go to join World War I, which started not long afterwards. (Most people did want to go, not then knowing how hellish and often pointless it would turn out to be, but Milne was a pacifist at the start. He went anyway, and hated it.) He had married just before the war and this produced the famous Christopher Robin, as in the stories. By the way, at prep school one of Milne's masters had been H G Wells, the *War of the Worlds* author who inspired Milne, and in later life he was a chum of Jeeves author P G Wodehouse – the admiration being mutual.

After the war, Milne was still mostly known for poetry, a lot of which was recycled stuff from his days at *Punch*. It wasn't until 1926 that the world first met the Bear of Very Little Brain, and the world just loved him straight away. The books have since been translated into 30 languages and still sell around a million a year round the world, *Vinnie Pookh* doing well in Russia, and surprise hit *Winnie Ille Pu* in Latin selling well in Britain and the United States. Like many writers, Milne admitted wishing for immortality, but not particularly through the bear. His creation has outgrown and outlived him: Milne died in 1956, and Christopher Robin in 1996, in the same month as Brian Staples who created the Latin version. Winnie-the-Pooh, however, is thriving. In fact, he's still hoping to finish his jar of honey before Piglet comes to tea.

WILLIAM DONALDSON (aka Henry Root) Brilliant prankster and all-round cad. If you read of someone's background as 'Winchester' (the great public school) and then 'Magdalene College, Cambridge' you might expect it to carry on with 'Brigade of Guards', or 'Leading surgeon', or 'Bishop of Oxford', or 'called to the Bar' or some such professional respectability.

In the case of William Donaldson, who died in 2005, it carried on with 'Serial adulterer', 'Crack head', 'Procurer of prostitutes', 'Failed novelist', 'Wilful prat' and 'Disastrous, awful impresario'. This utterly extraordinary outcome struck even that most *avant* of *gardes*, that most *noir* of *bêtes*, that most *terrible* of *enfants* theatre reviewer Kenneth Tynan as a bit rum – he described Donaldson as 'an old Wykehamist who ended up as a moderately successful Chelsea pimp'.

The reason most of us have heard of him, however, is his most brilliant creation, rampant Right-wing nutter and retired wet-fish merchant Henry Root. Under this alias he wrote to the great and the good, flattering their vanity with craven backside-licking and obviously absurd comments (obvious to everyone except those being flattered). This prompted the G&G to reply, making complete and utter fools of themselves in the process, and often exposing their self-centred pomposity, snobbery or vanity, which was a great service to the rest of us.

They made a fabulous book, *The Henry Root Letters*. Even better, he usually enclosed a cheque for one pound, which trivial amount was usually cashed by these often multi-millionaires, further exposing their true nature.

He told Margaret Thatcher (she cashed the £1 cheque) that Mary Whitehouse, the strident housewifely clean-up TV campaigner, should be made Home Secretary. He told the Queen he sympathised with the problems she was having with Princess Anne as: 'My Doreen, 19, has gone completely off the rails, so I know what it's like.' He asked the Tory party how much he'd have to donate to get a peerage (before this pretty well became a reality with both parties), and wickedly asked newsreader Angela Rippon to send him a photo of her even more beautiful arch-rival Anna Ford. When he wrote to right-wing tycoon and anti-European Sir James Goldsmith suggesting that Britain would be a better country if steps were taken to eliminate 'scroungers, perverts, Dutch pessary salesmen and Polly Toynbee' (a rather tediously right-on Left-wing columnist), Sir James wrote back and said he much appreciated Root's comments. This might tell us something about the late Sir James or it might illustrate how much notice the great and good really take of ordinary people's letters.

So when he told the head of the Metropolitan Police after yet another trial cock-up that it was 'better that ten innocent men be convicted than that one guilty man goes free', he was merely told: 'Your kind comments are appreciated.' Equally, when he told TV presenter Esther Rantzen she was 'a fat idiot' and her show 'a complete disgrace' he received a reply saying that 'hearing from viewers like yourself is a tremendous morale boost for all of us'.

He wrote to the Old Bailey: 'Now that the sensible practice of jury fixing is out in the open thanks to the irresponsible behaviour of the *Guardian*, I would like to nominate myself as a rigged juryman in certain trials. In cases involving pornographers, blasphemers and those prone to civil agitation and disorder, you'd have at least one vote under your belt …'

Donaldson grew up in the late 1930s in a Berkshire mansion with many servants, but his conscience seems to have been stirred at an early age when he heard his father had fired a chauffeur for voting Labour. When he arrived at public school his anarchic streak was already visible as, he later related, he vied for the title Stupidest Boy in School, only to be beaten by an unimaginably dim earl – the sort who goes: 'What? What? What? Fri'fully, fri'fully sorry, old boy, can't remember one's name.'

After a shaky career at Cambridge, Donaldson joined a famous advertising agency but walked out because they wanted him to write an ad for Ovaltine, which he loathed. He had inherited buckets of money, so in the early 1960s he set about becoming an impresario with various initially successful shows such as *Beyond The Fringe* (with Peter Cook, Dudley Moore, Jonathan Miller and Alan Bennett) and was also responsible for booking a completely unknown American singer called Bob Dylan (typically, he said it was 'the only way to get rid of the ******', who was sat in his office). However, after the middle of the 1960s his shows became increasingly disastrous. On one occasion he left the cast hanging around a north of England theatre unpaid with just a note saying: 'Have gone to London for money! Back tonight! Don't worry! We have a hit on our hands!' He never went back, of course. There was no money and no hit.

His personal life was impossibly complicated, involving more starlets, mistresses, elopements, blasphemy accusations, marriages, drugs, financial disasters and bankruptcies than the entire population of a fair-sized Scottish city, but it has to be said that some of the women involved were major actresses, such as Sarah Miles, or singers, such as Carly Simon. His dalliance with drugs went on for decades, although his position was not helped by his always taking the mickey out of the authorities. When his flat was raided by the drugs squad looking for cannabis and the officer cautioned him against saying anything that may be used in evidence, he replied: 'Haven't I seen you at one of my pot parties?'

His eccentric sexual arrangements don't need listing here but started in the bike shed at Winchester and continued via a Parisian professional to include every possible variation, involving two way-mirrors, fur coats, secretaries and video cameras. He even took the date-rape drug Rohypnol, he claimed, but said that as it always wiped his memory, he had to video himself to see what a good time he'd had.

He inherited the then fortune of £80,000 twice and lost it all; he made another fortune from the best-selling *Henry Root Letters* and lost all that too. When a journalist asked him how it had all gone, he replied: 'I've been a complete ****.' At one point, down to his last £2,000, he flew to Ibiza and spent it on a glass-bottomed boat, supposed to revive his fortunes. It sank, of course.

He said that, on the whole, he'd been deeply disappointed at his own behaviour in life, and told young people to study his life to avoid going wrong themselves. But the books are brilliant, and so, so rude. One eccentric touch was the insane cross-references in his book, some of which were too rude to repeat, but Magnus Magnusson, Sandi Toksvig, Mariella Frostrup and Sven-Goran Eriksson were all followed by 'See Eskimos working in the United Kingdom', which entry I couldn't find, of course.

If anyone ever, ever tells you again that National Service (that is the former conscription for a year or so in the military) made people fit into society, be responsible and know how to behave, quote William Donaldson. He served in submarines, and his common sense was totally torpedoed for life.

Sir,
I wish to protest most strongly about everything.

Henry Root, Park Walk, West Brompton.
Evening Standard Letters Page, Wednesday 15 August 1979

WILLIAM HORACE DE VERE COLE Cambridge University has the dubious honour of having produced the world's greatest prankster, April Fool purveyor par excellence, inveterate hoaxer by appointment to the Admiralty, the inimitable William Horace de Vere Cole (1881–1936).

De Vere Cole probably hoaxed people as a toddler, but he certainly brought his gift with him to Trinity College. In 1905 he darkened his appearance, dressed exotically and sent a telegram to the mayor, Alderman Spalding, saying that the Sultan of Zanzibar (who was in London for the coronation of Edward VII) was arriving at the station (or rather his uncle, a prince of Zanzibar). The mayor was put in a tizzy. The university was swamped with foreign visitors already for the 'Greek Question' – sorting out the language, not the place – and could not help. The chief constable who knew something about Africa was out of town.

What should the mayor do, as the reputation of Cambridge was at stake? It could not snub a visiting royal. The group (for the prince had a retinue including a translator) was met by an official welcoming party – well, a hurriedly called hansom cab and a waiter – and he and his entourage were wined, dined and shown the best sights the city and university had to offer. The sultan himself was detained in London to meet the king, the party explained, but the Prince of Zanzibar – de Vere Cole dressed up – was enthusiastic, but would converse only in 'Zanzibarian' as he was shown around King's, Caius and Trinity. Shown a bust of Queen Victoria, the prince bowed and exclaimed: 'Abba sti lacka burga!' which his translator duly rendered into something respectful. When the prince stubbed his toe, a columnist noted, the 'Zanzibarian' expletives seemed rather similar to English ones.

The local paper had only two weeks previously related a similar hoax back in 1873 when the arrival of the 'Shah of Persia' was met by the city band playing and the city's full regalia and dignitaries. De Vere Cole must surely have read that article, as would have the by-now suspicious dignitaries.

The 'prince', fearing exposure, made his apologies with many salaams and left by the next train (only to come back as an undergraduate on the return service.) The embarrassed university authorities could not find out which students had humiliated them – although one of their party went to the *Daily Mail* office in Fleet Street and gave the paper a great yarn (without naming all the perpetrators). It was not until de Vere Cole and his party had left Cambridge that they confessed. But it was merely a rehearsal for much greater things in Cole's whacky world.

Many of his pranks were well planned but others were brilliant, spur-of-the-moment numbers. For example, finding a ball of string in a London street, he asked a passing gentleman to hold one end while he measured something. He walked backwards around the corner unreeling it and asked another gentleman to hold tight to the other end, then walked off trying not to laugh out loud. How long the obliging chaps stood there is unknown.

Equally, he once came across a road crew waiting for instruction with their tools. He directed them to dig a trench at Piccadilly Circus, which caused mayhem until helpful police started directing traffic round the hole. Hours after de Vere Cole had gone the trench was still being dug.

Another time there was an awfully pretentious play put on in London's West End. Like the emperor's new clothes, no-one dared say what rubbish it was. De Vere Cole paid for eight seats across the front of the stalls, and had eight bald men sit there with one letter painted on top of each of their heads. It spelt out B*******, and the cast couldn't understand why gales of laughter from the circle seats and boxes above greeted the arrival of the eight bald latecomers.

Another time he was chatting to an MP near the Houses of Parliament and slipped his fob watch into the politician's pocket. De Vere Cole bet the man that he could beat him to the end of the street, and they promptly set off running. Cole fell behind and told a group of men 'Stop thief!' which in those days was enough to start a hue and cry. More people joined in and the shouting drew a police foot patrol, who stopped and searched the protesting MP, found the 'stolen' watch and were about to handcuff him when de Vere Cole owned up.

Even when on his honeymoon, in Venice in 1919, de Vere Cole couldn't let 1 April go without some form of gag. One night he sneaked off to the mainland where the streets, as in the rest of the world, were covered in horse manure, the traffic pollution of the day. He collected up a representative collection of the stuff and spread it around the Piazza San Marco in suitable piles – which must have seemed odd because no horse ever went there. What his bride thought of his preferred way of spending a honeymoon night is not recorded.

But his best prank was in February 1910, when he made a laughing stock of the Royal Navy, then the biggest fleet in the world, and in particular of its most powerful warship, HMS *Dreadnought*. He and his accomplices arrived at Portsmouth harbour only just after a message was delivered to the ship warning that the Emperor of Abyssinia was coming on an official visit. Some of them wore white robes and blackened faces, other were in top hats and tails as diplomats, and they carried an official telegram (forged) authorising the visit.

The captain hastily donned his best uniform and had the Royal Marines line up as a guard of honour. The 'emperor' and his party were piped aboard in traditional style and given a full VIP tour of the ship, showing off all the latest secret gunnery equipment, and ending in the wardroom with the best food and drink the navy could muster. The 'Abyssinians' talked in a strange language to each other – they were making it up as they went along – saying 'Bunga! Bunga!' enthusiastically every time they were shown something. One of the visitors was in fact a young woman called Virginia Stephen, later to be better known as author Virginia Woolf.

There was outrage and mockery in the press when the official party, having been taken back to the railway station, made their prank known. 'Bunga Bungle' was one headline, and over the next few days in Portsmouth, sailors were greeted with cries of 'Bunga! Bunga!' everywhere they went.

The humiliated admiralty sent the ship to sea until the fuss died down. The episode, known as the Bunga-Bunga Affair, was said to have highlighted security risks at a time of dangerous naval rivalry. It was also said by some to have epitomised the shallowness of the British imperial system, which, its critics would say, worked by sycophantic toadying to key foreigners who were gullible enough to fall for the soft-soap treatment. Alternatively, and more charitably to the navy, you could say it highlighted the way the British got where they were. They assembled the biggest empire ever seen and ran it peacefully with very few men – in the ratio of 1 to

250,000 in some countries – not by blasting off huge quantities of ammunition, as certain other powers would, but by good manners and being nice to the locals … whatever weird shape and form they came in. De Vere Cole wasn't an emperor or a sultan. But he was the prince of pranksters.

By 1965, the Cambridge city authorities had at last learned better. Someone calling himself the 'Shah of Persia' arrived at the city's airport, and some argued the bigwigs should ignore him and treat him like the second-rate imposter he clearly was. This was the real one, however.

CHRISTOPHER COCKERELL Eccentric inventor Sir Christopher Cockerell, 1910–99, of Peterhouse College, made the brilliant but nearly useless hovercraft. His father Sir Sydney Cockerell, a great typographer and bookbinder (and how apt his beautifully lettered gravestone at Grantchester, by the way), was curator of the Fitzwilliam Museum and so as a child Christopher met such greats as Bernard Shaw and Joseph Conrad. When T E Lawrence (of Arabia) visited, mechanically minded young Christopher was fascinated by his Brough Superior motorbike, the one that Lawrence was to die on not so many years later.

The boy's inventiveness served his country well in World War II when he devised navigation aids for bombers, saving many aircrew lives. After the war he went into pleasure craft – then enjoying a boom in East Anglia – and considered ways of reducing the friction between a speeding boat and the water. First he thought of air-bubble lubrication and then a cushion of air holding the craft out of the water entirely (actually a suggestion of Sir John Thornycroft in the previous century, who couldn't make it work). Cockerell famously made his first hovercraft out of a cocoa tin, a bucket and a vacuum cleaner.

Eventually huge four-engined hovercraft were crossing the English Channel carrying passengers and cars far faster than ferries, but the machines were expensive to run, not too pleasant to be on, and were overtaken by the Channel Tunnel and fast cat boats. They still run in some countries – and to the Isle of Wight – and are particularly good where sand and mud makes a conventional land or sea craft impracticable.

JEFFREY ARCHER The former Tory Party vice-chairman, globally successful novelist and disgraced jailbird let the impression rest that he was educated at Wellington and Brasenose, Oxford. Except that it wasn't the famous Wellington public school in Berkshire but a lesser school in Somerset; and his time at Brasenose was just a one-year diploma of education (during which Archer somehow ran for the university). So on this occasion he was more or less telling the truth. It would be like my letting it be known that I went to 'Dulwich and Cambridge'. Yes I did – but was thrown out of the third form of the former and merely did my A-levels at the Tech College in the latter after being thrown out of another school. I was far too thick/rebellious etc to make it to Cambridge.

Archer, who did for the British peerage what the Boston Strangler did for door-to-door salesmen, moved near to Cambridge – in fact at the Old Vicarage immortalised by Rupert Brooke at Grantchester – with his famously fragrant wife Mary, a scientist, although he has been happy to be associated more with Oxford.

Anyway, Archer kept us all amused for decades with his female connections, libel cases, astute share dealing and eventual jailing for perjury. What I can say in his defence is: What on earth did people expect? Hello, durbrain, he was known for one thing – creating fiction.

4 Eccentric Colleges

Top ten colleges and the weird characters who have peopled them

Symbols (1–5, the more the merrier)
☺ Eccentric/interesting people
🏰 Architecturally/historically interesting

CHRIST'S *Founded 1505* St Andrew's Street ☺ ☺ ☺ 🏰 🏰 🏰

Founded by Henry VII's mother, Lady Margaret Beaufort, who stipulated wisely that 'if any student or fellow do wipe his hande or fingers of the table clothe, he shall pay for every time one penny'. I hope it is still enforced, the current value being about £5. In fact, if she wants to pop round and have a word with my son … On the other hand, she lived at Christ's for a while and begged the dean not to whip students for certain misdemeanours.

Lady Margaret had a lot of fingers in a lot of pies and is a surprisingly central figure in European royalty. At the start of World War I, when there were a lot more crowned heads in Europe than there are now, Lady M was related to every one of them. Except King Zog of Albania, an oversight for which we will have to forgive her.

By the 18th century Christ's standards were going down the khazi. It was described as 'full of slumbering dons'. 'Fellows knew little and taught even less, dozing over port while waiting for college livings to fall vacant,' wrote one disenchanted tutor.

By the 1780s things were at a pretty pass. A student called Gunning complained that there were only three admissions in his year, and the other two could not read. He eventually became a bedell of the university and was told his only duties were to observe the statutes by breaking them and to carve well at table. The dons meanwhile spent their days drinking port, playing whist and eating. Things picked up a bit in the 19th century.

ALUMNI
Charles Calverley (1831–84), the poet, was a Christ's man, and left an indelible reputation for undergraduate excesses and eccentric behaviour behind him. In fact, he should have been at Balliol, Oxford, but had been sent down (expelled) for various japes such as throwing stones through the master's window (when it was closed) and ended up at Cambridge instead (neither the first nor last to do so).

A typical student prank of that day (and this) was when freshman Calverley stole the sign from the Green Man pub and ran back to the college pursued by the landlord and potman yelling abuse. He hid the sign under the bed and then joined the crowd below shouting up at the window. He was asked by the dean what all the noise was about, and was ready as ever with an apposite quotation: 'An evil and adulterous generation seeketh after a sign; and no sign shall be given it' (Matthew 12:39).

On another occasion Calverley walked across the sacred turf at another college, where the provost rebuked him. Calverley did not look sufficiently apologetic.

Provost: 'Do you know who I *am*?'

Calverley: 'No, sir, I do not.'

Provost, even more pompously: 'Look again, sir, and tell me what you see before you.'

Calverley: 'I see an elderly gentleman, apparently very irascible.'

An excellent reply (as was one once given in a mental hospital to someone bossy from the government saying indignantly: 'Do you know who I *am*?' which was 'No, dear, but ask the nurses and they'll tell you'.).

Calverley is today more remembered for his unsparing and brilliant parodies of Victorian favourite poets such as Tennyson and Browning in *Fly Leaves* (1872), and by golly, they needed lampooning. He became known as the 'Prince of Parodists'. Calverley wrote a rather good (in a light, G K Chestertonish way) poem *Beer* which expressed astonishment that the ancient Greeks can have achieved anything without ale.

Milton (the blind poet, not the nappy steriliser) was a bit miserable at Christ's (now there's a surprise) and was nicknamed the 'lady of Christ's' because of his girlish complexion. He described his studies as 'an asinine feast of sow thistles and brambles' and was whipped by his tutor. Not nearly enough, clearly.

Charles Darwin, who changed most people's world view utterly through his theory of evolution by natural selection (rather than Creation). He started his naturalist hobby early, and once while at Cambridge he was capturing beetles to study and popped one in his mouth to hold it while using his hands to bottle a second one. The one in his mouth promptly showed Darwin it had evolved a jolly useful defence mechanism – by ejecting a foul-tasting acid. By the way, Darwin had previously had a false start as a medical student at Edinburgh, which suggests that every student should be allowed at least one change of direction.

Richard Whiteley, presenter of a much-loved British afternoon TV quiz show called *Countdown*, died in 2005. Whiteley came over as a genial old cove in his blazer and tie, joshing with co-presenter Carol Vorderman. In fact, he had secret mistresses, a love child, hidden properties and all kinds of complications that would make you want to avoid being executor of his will. The lovable Uncle Richard was a bit of a Dirty Dick.

Other alumni include controversial Ali G and Borat comedian **Sacha Baron Cohen**; Inspector Morse (and Oxford-loving) creator **Colin Dexter**; 'perfect face for radio' politician **David Mellor**; **Earl Mountbatten**, last viceroy of India, blown to shreds by the IRA on his yacht; historian **Simon Schama**; South African leader **Jan Smuts**; Archbishop of Canterbury **Rowan Williams**.

CLARE Founded 1326 Trinity Lane ☺ ☺ ☺ 🏛 🏛 🏛

Second-oldest and named after a woman ... called Elizabeth. Well, founded as University Hall in 1326 and refounded by one Elizabeth de Clare in 1338, to replace clerks (clergy) killed by the plague. She was driven to charity by being thrice widowed, and the college's arms are black-edged with gold tears to recall this. The elegant buildings we see today are largely 17th century, as the original burnt down in 1362 and 1521 (so the next one is well overdue). At the south end of Trinity Lane, off Trinity Street. Extravagant confection of a gatehouse which looks like a mad Jacobean wedding cake. Note the fan vaulting as you go through. On the right is the chapel, with a very odd and heavily decorated octagonal antechapel. In the chapel is a window to Protestant pioneer Hugh Latimer (see *Alumni*).

The library contains 35 *incunabula* (books printed before 1500). It's not a word you often come across, but the singular *incunabulus* means, I think, in the cradle – metaphorically in the infancy of printing. If you're ignorant like me you'll realise that you didn't need to know that, but are nevertheless glad you do. Not to be confused with an *incubus* which is some kind of devilish thing that likes to have sex with sleeping women. I have no idea if the college has many of those.

The hall is also on this north side. The gate on the far (west) side leads to **Clare Bridge** over the Cam, a very fine bridge built in 1638 and decorated with 16 stone balls, one of which has a wedge cut out, the theory being that the builder's pay was one shilling short so he removed a bit in protest.

Clare Bridge can be called Catchpole Bridge because students like to catch the poles of punting tourists from this bridge, so beware as you go under. The wags. An even better jape was when they made an extra stone ball out of foam, and painted it to match the others. As a punt headed underneath, the students heaved with much apparent effort this ball off the balustrade. As it fell, the panic-stricken occupants of the punt leapt overboard. The lightweight ball bounced harmlessly out of the punt and drifted down the river, according to Robert Kenny (see page 109).

Modern students aren't much more sensible. This was recounted to me: It was a scene tailor-made for alumnus **David Attenborough** when tell-tale noises were heard among the branches of a large willow at Clare College. You can imagine him whispering to camera: 'There, almost invisible to the untrained eye among the branches of the venerable old tree, are the two entwined bodies, shrouded in darkness but unmistakably performing the classic courtship ritual.' Venturing to investigate in temperatures scarcely above zero, the night porter was bemused when a naked young woman dropped to the ground, let out a moan, rubbed her back then calmly picked up her cast-aside clothing to get dressed again. Moments later her companion followed and the newly clothed couple – without a word of explanation – slid off into the shadows. A double first, probably.

ALUMNI

William Butler did for constipation what Vlad the Impaler did for human rights. A medical quack and physician to James I, his legacy was for years known widely as *Dr Butler's Purging Ale*. This evil concoction, made by hanging a thin bag containing senna, polypody of oak, very strong spices, agrimony, maidenhair and scurvy grass in a barrel of strong ale, had a violently laxative effect, likened by its victims to the discharge of the largest cannon used in the navy. He probably wouldn't have come to much had he not been approached by King James, who was suffering from an agonising bad back his doctors could not cure. Butler prescribed a barrel of his purging ale – as he did for most patients – and whatever happened to the king, he forgot entirely about his back. In gratitude, King James conferred a degree upon Butler and appointed him court physician, which went down with the other doctors like a dose of something very unpleasant.

Butler's eccentric treatments were deeply unorthodox. For the relief of epilepsy, he would ask a patient to sit still and close his eyes, then fire a pair of pistols either side of his head, inches from his ears. For malaria or the ague, then common, he would throw patients into the Thames head first. For opium overdose he had a man inserted in the freshly killed belly of a cow. The rich queued up to be so treated.

Hugh Latimer, the Protestant cleric who gets burnt at Oxford in 1555 in 'Bloody' Mary's brief Catholic revival, became for ever after known as one of the famous Oxford martyrs despite being a Cambridge man.

Charles, Lord Cornwallis as commander-in-chief managed to lose the American War of Independence and then become Governor-General of India (d 1805). The Americans don't seem to have held this against Clare, with links to Yale flourishing.

Nicholas Ferrar set up an idealistic Christian community at Little Gidding, near Huntingdon in 1626, which was destroyed by the Puritans in the Civil War, and visited by American poet T S Eliot in 1936, giving rise to his last poem, one of the *Four Quartets*, called *Little Gidding*. A window in the chapel celebrates Ferrar.

William Whitehead, Britain's worst poet laureate, from 1757 to 1785, was a fellow of Clare.

Other alumni Somewhat better World-War-I poet **Siegfried Sassoon**; modern composer **John Rutter**; scientist **James Watson**, one half of the Crick & Watson DNA partnership; and a chap called **W H 'Fluffy' Fulford** who in the 20th century failed to endear himself to his wife, or women everywhere, by telling friends: 'Honeymoons are all very nice in their way, but after a few days a man longs for a little intelligent conversation.'

What does this place celebrate in its name? That a member of an unpleasant family of self-serving political turncoats and despised, greedy landlords made one of the world's worst marriages. And yes, how did you guess, it is Downing as in 10 Downing Street, London.

George Downing was a ruthless Puritan representative of Cromwell during the Civil War and the Commonwealth (a sort of republic) that followed, with ambassador-like functions in Europe and based in The Hague, careful to voice the politically current views against the monarchy. Yet when he saw the way the wind was blowing he made secret contact with Charles II, and the minute the monarchy was restored in 1660, he was all over the king, professing his loyalty and love of the monarchy and the Church of England, and indeed building Downing Street, home of the prime minister today. It worked, and he was granted considerable estates as well as the title of baronet. The later Sir George Downing of Gamlingay Park, Cambridgeshire, who ended up founding Downing College, was that first baronet's grandson.

This Downing was as deeply unpleasant as his grandfather but his greatest misfortune was to undergo an arranged marriage when he was 15 and the girl, a cousin, 13. They couldn't stand each other (which reflects well on the young lady) and parted with the marriage unconsummated. He went on a grand tour of Europe for a year or so, as the gentry did, and then Lady Downing was sent, with her parents' connivance, to be a maid of honour (resident companion) at Queen Anne's court, which made Sir George refuse to speak with her as he had made her promise to stay at home.

She waited ten years for him to forgive her but in desperation sought for the marriage to be annulled, which any reasonable Church would surely have done, as they had never spent a night together, nor wanted to. She was styled 'neither maid, wife, nor widow'. Sir George did not resist, admitting that 'disgusts and aversions' between them were so strong that no mutual agreement could ever be reached. The bishops who had to judge this refused, however, and the miserable Downings continued with their titles and sham marriage until their dying day.

So, obviously, no children. What to do with the large estates? Sir George left them to three cousins, one after the other, with the proviso that if they too died childless the money would found a Cambridge college, clearly not likely. And this is what eventually happened, although not until after a horrendous lawsuit by some other more distant greedy members of the family. This third Sir George Downing died in 1749 yet the college didn't open for business until 1821, which even by the standards of the insane, cumbersome legal system Dickens satirised in *Bleak House*, was quite some law case.

The college was now hitting the full-on Greek Revival architecturally (pity they didn't delay another 30 years and it would have gone back to Gothic, fans of the latter style may think) and a massive grand court in this style was designed to outdo both Trinity and King's. Built on land between Trumpington Street and Regent Street, it would dominate the view for those arriving from London. In the event, the money ran out, not least because so much had been squandered on lawyers. An attractive classical building was nevertheless erected (as George III had requested), though not nearly as large as planned, and later additions have kept to the original style, including the very fine Maitland Robinson library, full-on Greek revival in style, although in fact it's younger than Britney Spears.

The road across the front of site became Downing Street, which at least gave various people lucky enough to live there an impressive address (including myself, but sadly not at number ten). But few of those who lived there ever knew that the whole thing hinged on the most miserable marriage imaginable, and a family rightly detested by all who knew them.

In spite of all that background, Downing rapidly became known for gentle, kind, polite and mild masters and dons. Mostly.

ALUMNI Theatre director **Trevor Nunn**; **Basil Fawlty** (well, John Cleese, whose famous Ministry of Silly Walks was said to have been inspired by Downing types avoiding the puddles on the paths); actress **Thandie Newton** (it is thpelt like that); cricketer **Mike Atherton**; radio chap **Brian Redhead**; BNP chairman **Nick Griffin**; film maker **Michael Winner**.

GONVILLE AND CAIUS Founded 1348 ☺ ☺ ☺ ♜ ♜

Known as Caius, pronounced keys. The double name is because it was founded twice – once by Edmund Gonville, a Norfolk rector in 1348, just in time,

LET'S ELEVATE THE GUTTER

'Is this the brainiest graffiti in the country?' asked the newspapers when a spectacularly boffiny bit of artwork appeared on a Cambridge road recently. I have to say, as a pedant, it would be a graffito, graffiti being plural, so the newspapers weren't that brainy, but this one was exceptional even for a city where I remember the words 'Exams kill by degrees' once painted up in Downing Street.

This graffito's siting was also most apposite, as it was on the roadway outside the Cavendish laboratory where DNA was first discovered as the code of all life in 1953. The drawing was of a complex molecule called guanine, one of the bases of DNA. As it's quite a narrow road, clearly the whole thing wouldn't fit. The eventual product of Crick and Watson & co's famous discovery was the human genome, published in 2000, but that would need a slightly wider and longer road, having (I'm told) three billion letters of genetic code, which would fit nicely on that road that goes from the top to the bottom of the Americas (both gutters).

It all makes a pleasant change from yellow lines. As it's Cambridge, how about replacing all, or at least some, of the yellow lines with parking according to intelligence and knowledge instead of boring time and money? Solve the maths equation, the bit of Greek, or the chemical formula painted in the gutter (and frequently changed) and you park all day. If you can't, get on yer bike. I'd have to come by bike, of course …

inconveniently, for the Black Death, and then again by Dr John Caius in 1557, just in time, conveniently, for the equals sign to be invented in mathematics. (A lot of sums must have been waiting to be finished, one supposes.) It was just as well that Dr Caius came along because the place had become terribly run down: its beer had been raided by the men of St Gerard's Hostel, cattle wandered though the college, frogs and rats lived in the buildings, property had been lost and squandered. Dr Caius put an end to all that, although his rule was somewhat stern. For example, he provided in the statutes that no scholars were to be elected who were 'deaf, dumb, deformed, lame, chronic invalids, or Welshmen'.

This would seem not only to rule out much of the Labour party (some on more than one count) but be as insulting to Welshmen as TV-quiz-show-host Anne Robinson who once said 'What is Wales *for*?' to annoy a Welsh contestant. Despite a cheerful willingness to annoy a certain kind of po-faced professional Welshman, and despite being a small bit Welsh myself (a Welsh rare bit, as it were), I have my doubts about this word meaning Welsh as in the modern principality. Didn't 'Welsh' just mean foreign once? It could just mean no *foreigners* (which would, of course, be almost as great a loss). Perhaps Dr Caius had an aversion to foreign food, all that garlic and curry. After all, he asked for the college to have a three-sided court 'lest the air from being confined within a narrow space should become foul'. Sounds like a Cambridge man who has had to share digs with a curry nut.

ALUMNI I rather like the high-minded comment on the college's website:

> It is not possible, nor desirable, to produce a definitive list of famous Caians [as members of Caius College are known]. Fame is a very subjective measure, and 650 years of College history yield a large number of Caians. By concentrating too much on 'famous' people, one risks forgetting those who have made, and still make, the College a vibrant community.

Well said! Good for them. None of this vacuous celebrity culture for them. I bet they don't read *Hello!* magazine (*Goodbye!* magazine in which celebs come to ghastly ends might be more fun). Oh fickle finger of fame, empty-headed bastard brother of snobbery! You know the guff: 'I had to remind the waiter who we *were*. Is he *anybody*? Now he is *somebody*.' Too, too ghastly …

On the other hand, snobbery has a point. Fame *used* to be awarded for considerably better reasons than today's 'I slept with three well fit footballers, dinneye, a Cabinet minister and a goat so I deserve my own TV show, innit, and a Sunday paper column, written for me because I'm too fick, inneye'. Yuck and double yuck.

So, shame-facedly admitting that we're human and swayed by fame after all, here goes with some of the great & the good of G&C …

William Harvey, who discovered the circulation of the blood (called 'crack-brained' for his ideas expressed in *The Circulation of the Blood* and other works in, er, a similar vein); **Edward Wilson**, the doctor on Scott's disastrous expedition to the Antarctic, who died with him in that heroic failure (you can see his flag in the hall); **Harold Abrahams**, the *Chariots of Fire* runner (page 30); **Francis Crick**, one half of Crick & Watson who discovered the secrets of DNA and won a Nobel Prize; **Stephen Hawking**, robotic-voiced wheelchair-bound author who triumphed brilliantly over his disability to write the *Brief History of Time;* Downing Street spinmeister **Alastair Campbell**, about whom I'd better say absolutely nothing; vile perjurer **Titus Oates** (not the companion of Wilson above – that Oates was Lawrence, although nicknamed Titus after this 17th century charlatan); oily TV presenter **David 'Hello, good evening and welcome' Frost**; Labour MP **Keith Vaz**. You begin to see why they didn't want to boast.

Unfamous Caius men include **W Philcox**, winner of the 1921 Oxford and Cambridge air race, when six biplanes, three with tails in Cambridge blue and three in Oxford's darker blue, raced round a 120-mile course. One aviator, a Mr Pring of New College, Oxford, failed to complete the course, coming down midway and hitting some railings. The headline could have been 'Pring prong prang'.

JESUS *Founded 1496* Jesus Lane ☺ ☺ ☺ 🏰 🏰 🏰

Originally 'the College of the Blessed Mary the Virgin, St John the Evangelist, and the glorious Virgin St Radegund' which double mention of virginity may or may not reflect on its current inhabitants, but certainly didn't at the time. It had been a nunnery of St Radegund until it was visited in 1496 by the exceedingly pious not to say virtuous Bishop of Ely, John Alcock. He was appalled to find two nuns of ill repute locally (one of them pregnant and we're not talking virgin birth). The bishop accused the nuns of 'improvidence, extravagance and incontinence' (so *definitely* not like the current lot then) and changed the place into a college. The college coat of arms or flag consequently proudly bears three cocks because the bishop's name was Alcock (the birds, that is).

Apart from that, it was the usual Cambridge pattern of 16th-century religious oppression, 17th-century Civil War bungling, 18th-century decadent, drunken idleness and 19th-century recovery of standards, 20th-century slaughter in two world wars and 21st-century – well, we shall have to wait and see.

ALUMNI

Thomas Cranmer, Archbishop of Canterbury and Jesus college fellow, in the 16th century was famously burnt for his faith at Oxford in the Catholic v Protestant oppression. While at Cambridge he married a relative of the landlady of the Dolphin Inn (as you do, particularly if she's pregnant by you) and therefore would have been excluded from holy orders (and was duly kicked out of being a fellow at Jesus) had she not died in childbirth soon afterwards (upon which he was readmitted as if nothing had happened). All a bit rum when you remember that Cranmer is considered by many as the founder of the whole Church of England.

Cranmer's elevation to greatness came in a fascinating way. He fled the plague in Cambridge in 1529 and was staying in Essex near where the king was lodged. King

Henry VIII was wrangling with the question of how to divorce Catherine of Aragon when the pope wouldn't let him. Cranmer offered the opinion locally that there was a legal way to avoid asking the pope. The king heard of this and, never one to mess about on the marital (or indeed martial) front, sent for him, saying: 'Let him be sent for out of hand. This man, I trow, has got the right sow by the ear.' Thus his path to greatness was secured. What a nice chap.

In the next century the college unwisely sided with the king in the Civil War and, after he lost, most dons fled (after burying the chapel organ in the grounds).

Laurence Sterne, author of *Tristram Shandy*, is the nomination for 18th-century decadence. Sterne was particularly lazy at the college and in 1733 used to lie under a walnut tree in Cloister Court, later wrote:

> At Cambridge many years ago,
> In Jesus was a Walnut tree;
> The only thing it had to show,
> The only thing folk went to see …

Samuel Taylor Coleridge, romantic poet, was in 1791 an even worse student than Sterne, drinking and carousing with mighty disrespect. Once, when someone went to help the drunken Coleridge, who was flailing about in a gutter next to an equally helpless friend, he called out: 'Leave me, help my friend, he can't swim!'

On another occasion Coleridge wanted to disrupt some disciplinary proceedings against a friend in the Senate House. He chose a seat at the back behind a man with no arms. At the point where he agreed with something, Coleridge clapped loudly and quickly disappeared. The proctor fought his way to the seat and angrily accused the student of clapping. The poor student stood up and shook his coat off, saying: 'Alas, sir, would that were possible!'

Coleridge also had to flee Cambridge because of his debts at one point and joined the King's Regiment of Light Dragoons as Silas Tomkins Cumberback (well, it saved getting luggage with different initials, I suppose) but was soon back at Cambridge, which he left without a degree. Actually he was rather good at not finishing stuff, as with his wonderful poem *Kubla Khan*, an opium-trance work which was annoyingly interrupted and not finished (so it should be Kubla Khan't).

Lewis Gordon Pugh, law graduate solicitor, like many people, just loves to take a dip. Unlike most people the eccentric lawyer does it by diving off icebergs into water at 0°C, to the astonishment of onlookers – penguins, seals and the odd killer whale mostly.

Lewis, 36 in 2006, has taken the record for the most southerly swims. He hates the idea of wearing a wetsuit or the traditional goosefat covering to protect himself from the icy waters, and wears nothing but some Speedo trunks and a swimming cap, and yet managed a plunge of 18 minutes 10 seconds, thus entering the record books. Doctors say he has an odd ability to increase his internal body temperature before he starts. Just looking at all the ice and water makes his body temperature soar by 2°, his face flushes, and he begins to sweat profusely despite being fit and slim. His heart rate doubles.

They have called the condition 'anticipatory thermogenesis' – the creation of heat. He trains in a pool filled with half a ton of ice cubes.

Puzzled doctors found that while he should have contracted dangerous hypothermia after each Antarctic swim, his core temperature was still elevated.

Lewis, born in Plymouth, Devon, but raised in South Africa, has also gained the record for the most northerly swim of 1km round the northern tip of Spitsbergen at 80°N, and swam the entire 204km length of Norway's longest fiord in 21 days.

Alistair Cooke, the amazingly long-lived BBC radio journalist who brought us his programme *Letter From America* for a staggering 58 years until his death in 2004 aged 95, should not be forgotten amongst the Jesus alumni. Cooke went to America in the 1930s and presented memorable jazz programmes which wowed British audiences with a whole new, daring, this-joint-is-jumpin' kind of music. Yet he was still there through the war (becoming American in 1941), with his increasingly gentle and grandfatherly delivery, *still* there when each Kennedy was shot (right there in one case, next to the body), and *still* there when the Twin Towers came down, and still broadcasting a month before his death. His smooth delivery belied the fact that he made no script for his show which brought an incisive and witty analysis of what was good and bad about America to 50 countries every week. It is the longest-running series in history presented by one person (although with luck English eccentric Patrick Moore may soon be giving it a run for its money with his *Sky at Night* programme).

The honours Cooke received were huge: an honorary knighthood from the Queen; being a guest on the *Muppet Show* and being asked to address the US Congress on its 200th anniversary. There, having initially said he was a bit lost for words and felt naked, he drew himself up to his full height and said: 'I accept your nomination for President of the United States!'

Other alumni Others who didn't do things include **Nick Hornby** who didn't invent model railways but is a modern novelist; **Prince Edward** who didn't become a marine; and **Thomas Malthus**, the early 19th-century economist who is said to have given that subject the title of 'the dismal science' but didn't. He argued that famine, pestilence and disease would always correct the tendency of man to outbreed the available food supply. So far, he has been wrong.

KING'S *Founded 1441* King's Parade ☺ ☺ ☺ 🏠 🏠 🏠 🏠 🏠

Famously described as a chapel with a small college attached, such is the magnificence of the building made famous by the annual Christmas Eve service (see page 191).

Founded by Henry VI to receive boys from his school, Eton College, it still does, although others are let in from time to time. Henry had a warren of medieval shops, lanes, paths, wharves, cottages and even a church flattened to clear the bank of the Cam at this point, which is difficult to imagine as one looks from a punt at the pristine lawns, college and chapel. College rules forbid bringing monkeys, foxes, bears, stags or badgers into the grounds and also ban wrestling in chapel (apart from spiritual wrestling, of course). Henry VII continued the building work but famously stayed away from the laying of his foundation stone because of the 'aier and the Paestilence'.

Much more recently, Charlie Carter, who worked at Eton College, came to King's to collect money he said was due to him from scholars for the use of various boats, guns and victuals. Undergraduate Harry Matthews suggested they give him a wine party while they discussed the debts, and got Charlie hopelessly drunk. He was sewn up inside an old greatcoat and taken to the mail coach office. The snoring bundle, properly labelled, was taken to London and the guard bribed to put him on the Windsor coach so he could be eventually dropped off at Eton. The boys there liberated Charlie from the coat and he emerged with a very sore head, never to bother King's men again.

King's Chapel has always attracted that eccentric Cambridge breed, roof climbers. Banners, traffic cones, and other items have been put on pinnacles that would have tested Edmund Hillary and Sherpa Tensing. One brolly was put on a particularly inaccessible one in 1932, so porters summoned a huntin', shootin' and fishin' undergraduate to blast it down with a shotgun, which he did. The next day there was a Union Jack there, but the same student refused to fire on his own flag, so a steeplejack had to be called out. Famously, in 1965 anti-war students strung a huge banner calling for 'Peace in Vietnam' – and then cheekily complained about the dangerous stonework.

ALUMNI Alumni include **Rupert Brooke**, war poet (more on page 33); novelists **E M Forster**, **J G Ballard**, **Zadie Smith** and first British prime minister **Robert Walpole**.

Eccentric **Oscar Browning**, who should have been known as 'Gravy' Browning, 1837–1923, was a bon viveur/gourmet par excellence without becoming a snob or a slob. He seemed to eat or drink most of the time, and set his alarm clock for 03.00 so he could down a bottle of stout and fall asleep again. He became Master of Eton College (which he left after an inappropriate relationship of some sort) and returned to Cambridge as a history don, writing several histories of European states and royal families, many of whom he had visited on his travels. He described the emperor of the Austro-Hungarian Empire as the 'nicest emperor I have ever met'.

This Bunter-like approach to food was obviously common in that era. In the 1920s, King's did rather well in the rowing races, the bumps. Telegrams and letters flooded in from older Kingsmen protesting at this unseemly heartiness.

MAGDALENE *Founded 1428* Magdalene Street ☺ ☺ ☺ ☺ ☺ 🏰 🏰 🏰

Founded, or rather refounded, by notorious wheeler-dealer Thomas Audley who had made vast amounts of money looting the monasteries at their dissolution in the early 16th century. He is said to have considered that the college name – pronounced and indeed originally spelt Maudleyn – contained his own name, and had changed it to this from the previous Buckingham College. If you suspect, by the way, that Audley had to do with the stately home Audley End nearby, that even has its own railway station on the line to Liverpool Street, you would be right – it was his home.

The college was frankly known for drunkenness and laxity for most of its history. Cows and hunting dogs were often kept in the court, books were overgrown with mould through disuse and a valuable gift of seven acres in the City of London was disposed of in a scandalous manner (but the college gets its revenge – see page 200). In the 19th century things got a little more studious, and tea replaced booze, to the point where it was jested that the Cam at Magdalene was said to be becoming unnavigable due to mountains of tea leaves thrown in.

ALUMNI
Samuel Pepys, the outwardly respectable bureaucrat of Restoration England whose secret diary, written in a strange shorthand was not decoded until 1819. It revealed him to be a far more lecherous, cynical and devious character. He had been a sizar

(poor student) on arrival at Magdalene in 1650 (just after Charles I's head was chopped off) and was soon described by the college as being 'scandalously overseene in drink'. Funny how even the poorest students can *always* find enough money for a booze-up. He started his famous diary in 1660, the year Charles II restored the monarchy. Pepys's diary and library was eventually left, complete with bookcases made for it, to the college, and is kept in the order which he arranged it – by size, smallest first. How much more fun than alphabetical. He also insisted that the collection stay exactly as he left it, with no more or fewer books. No Enid Blyton, then.

Charles Kingsley, the author of *The Water Babies*, had a degree examination which showed just how bad 19th-century Magdalene had become. He was asked to show the workings of a village pump and could not; instead he drew a pump in a village green with children skipping about. For this, he was given an upper second!

Other alumni include **George Mallory**, who climbed Everest in 1924 'because it was there' and may have reached the top before dying there (where he will indeed ever rest); founder of an acting dynasty **Sir Michael Redgrave** who arrived at Magdalene in 1927 and whose films included *The Dam Busters* and *The Go-Between*; **C S Lewis**, he of *The Lion, the Witch and the Wardrobe*, was a fellow after moving from the Magdalen in Another Place; writer and TV brainbox **Bamber Gascoigne**; mid-20th-century Archbishop of Canterbury **Michael Ramsey**; **Kenneth 'round the' Horne**;

designer **Norman Hartnell**; satyrist and satirist **William 'Henry Root' Donaldson** (see page 56); BBC foreign editor and 'liberator of Kabul' **John Simpson**.

If this suggests that the college blossomed and bore fruit in the mid 20th century where it had previously been a miserable, manky twig, that's about right.

A less well-known but eccentric Magdalene man died aged 90 in 2005: war hero **Myles Hildyard.** Captured in the aftermath of the invasion of Crete, Hildyard, a captain with the Notts Yeomanry (Sherwood Rangers), heard that the Germans were to fly all Allied officers off the island to mainland prison camps. He persuaded a fellow PoW that if they wore bright-blue hospital coats and carried buckets and spades, no-one would believe they were trying to escape. They walked out of the camp safely but then met two Germans. They chatted to them and, as planned, the Germans assumed they had a right to be there and couldn't be trying to escape in that get-up. After many adventures in the mountains, they managed to reach Turkey in a fishing boat 90 days later. They reached British forces in Cairo by going through Smyrna, Damascus and Jerusalem. They were both awarded the MC for their daring escape, although Hildyard's parents knew nothing of his exploits.

Earlier, Hildyard had advised them to put exploding Friesian cows in their fields as booby traps for German parachutists, but he failed to tell them he had escaped from Crete and survived. When the family bank manager said: 'Oh yes, he's alive and drawing cheques over there' they realised he was alive and free. His mother fainted. Hildyard fought his way across North Africa, landed at D-Day in Normandy, fought his way across Europe and took part in the German surrender of Hamburg. He then returned to Flintham Hall, the family manor house in Nottinghamshire, and made running it his life's work. He installed a dazzling white copy of Michelangelo's statue of David at one end of the swimming pool.

QUEENS' *Founded 1448 Silver Street* ☺ 🏰 🏰

Probably the only college in the known universe whose *raison d'être*, whose *sine qua non*, whose *cri de coeur*, whose *joie de vivre*, whose *éclat et élan*, whose *mas que nada*, whose *esprit de corps*, whose *je ne sais quoi* is … that humblest of punctuation marks, the apostrophe. Founded in 1448 by the wife of Henry VI and given further support by the wife of Edward IV in 1465, who gave Queen's new endowments and statutes, at which point the apostrophe moved beyond the s to make it Queens' (as there were two queens) which differentiates it from Oxford's Queen's. Allegedly.

Not that it is unimportant. Fussing over how many queens are allowed would, of course, be quite normal in some places in Cambridge I've been to, and fussing over apostrophes is what sub-editors do for a living. And apostrophes aren't trivial: graduates of Queens' are after all unlikely to join the less literate greengrocers of Britain who advertise 'avocado's, £1.50'. In fact, Queen Elizabeth II has recently supported the college, which has led to an increase in their already considerable pride at their royal patronesses, if not in apostrophes.

So far, so pedantic, although if truth be known Henry VI Part One and his chums couldn't have cared less about apostrophes, if there were any: spelling was very fluid.

Nobody took the slightest bit of notice until the 19th century when punctilious, picky, pettifogging, poltroonious pedants took over and moved the apostrophe.

Erasmus, perhaps their most famous alumnus, wrote about the place which he rather loathed (the feeling was mutual), in Latin, of course, as *Collegium Reginae* (the college of one queen) whereas being the scholar he was (understatement) he would surely have written *Collegium Reginarum* had he meant the college of two (or indeed a great number of) queens.

The correct title of the college, it pompously tells us, is: 'The Queen's College of St Margaret and St Bernard, commonly called Queens' College, in the University of Cambridge.'

Has that cleared up this absolute aberration of appallingly approximate apostrophic apoplexy? No, I thought not. Let's talk *commonly* and settle for Queens'.

From the punter's point of view, Queens' is the college whose parts are joined by the famed **Mathematical Bridge**, or Wooden Bridge, as the college calls it somewhat prosaically. How great an achievement is the Mathematical Bridge? It seems to be a solution to a test where you are given a pile of lolly sticks and, instead of building a model of the *Titanic* to put in the bath with the soap as an iceberg, are asked to

94

bridge a gap two lolly sticks wide. If that is the case, you may ask, aren't all bridges not comprised of one long log or slab of stone mathematical: the Romans made fantastic arches, which still stand, out of small bits of stone, after all. Aren't they mathematical? By the way, *don't* whatever you do step on to the Hypothetical Bridge three yards upstream. It really isn't there.

But there was more to the Mathematical Bridge, built in 1749. It was made of cleverly constructed pieces that were put together as a kit without nails or screws and could be taken down and presumably re-erected anywhere. This became a problem, as students were fond of taking it to bits and then forgot how to put it together again. Dons were left with a kit of parts to puzzle over, a bit like Ikea furniture. For this reason the authorities reluctantly bolted it together, not because it needed bolts to stand up. Or so the legend says – another don insists the screws are structural. I am also told the woodwork has been replaced from time to time, so you're not crossing the actual 1749 timbers. It's like the road sweeper who swears he used the same broom for 50 years – "Onest, guv, I only replaced the brush 'ead five times and the 'andle six times.'

I read somewhere that the design was good because it meant it could be taken down quickly in the event of a German invasion in 1940. How absolutely ludicrous. I mean it was bad enough blowing holes in seaside piers, many of which never recovered, but what German army was going to use this little wooden bridge made of lolly sticks to rush its panzers from one half of Queens' to another?

The bridge was said by someone to join the 15th century with the 20th, and the newer part on the west bank had the novelty of baths for the students and dons. One of the latter objected to the baths being a profligate expense, as students were 'only up for eight weeks at a time'. It rather reminds me of a northern working-class man who said proudly: 'Dad had a bath every summer, even if he didn't need one.'

ALUMNI Archbishops, ambassadors and governors of just about everywhere (including an ambassador to *Scotland* which must have been a while ago) and heaps of lawyers.

Desiderius Erasmus (1466–1536) mentioned above is claimed as a great alumnus, but although yes he was brilliant, witty, learned, etc, there is little direct evidence that this great humanist and father of the Renaissance and Reformation was a member of the college, more that he stayed here while in Cambridge. He loathed Cambridge's people who, he said, 'combine extreme boorishness with extreme bad faith' and surpassed the English in general for being inhospitable. (Not *at all* like today, then.) He complained about the college wine being almost vinegar, and how the burning of heretics was putting up the price of firewood (ah, there's compassion for you) although it is hard at this distance to know if that was a bad taste joke.

Apart from Razzy, there are not really many people you'd particularly admire or look up to, and a few types you'd avoid like the plague.

T H White (d1963), wrote a novel *Darkness at Pemberley* which was set in Queens' or somewhere very like it. As a child, I loved his *Once and Future King* (he was into all that Arthurian stuff big time). White said he disliked his tutor at Queens' 'to the point of rage for about a year'.

Sir Ranulph 'Rasher' Bacon became deputy commissioner of the Metropolitan Police. In the 1960s he controversially advised the public to 'have a go' at criminals (thus engendering many a 'Have a go hero' headline) and said that a shot-gun 'is part of the adult Englishman's equipment' and useful for deterring criminals. But back then it wasn't so odd: coppers used to nab villains rather than blather on about multicultural inclusiveness, community outreach delivery and sexuality issues as if they were vicars or social workers.

Charlie Falconer, the chubby unelected Lord Chancellor who is no doubt so unfairly dubbed one of Tony's cronies, although he *has been* a chum of Mr Blair, and is indelibly linked with that catastrophe of New Labour profligacy, the Millennium Dome.

Stephen Fry (b1957), actor and comedian, recreated Oscar Wilde in the film. Very, very clever but not quite as brilliant as he thought himself (Wilde or Fry, you decide). Sometimes a little preciously smug – Fry stormed off abroad somewhere from a West End show that received bad reviews once, although not quite as far as ...

Michael Foale, first British man into space (with the help of NASA).

So those are Queens' great achievements: I mean, if you had produced Charlie Falconer and Stephen Fry, you would admit to it only under torture, not boast about it, wouldn't you?

The president of the college at the time of writing is one **Baron Eatwell**, which sounds like someone fat made up by Dickens but is, of course, just the title of a perfectly respectable academic. The president lives in a half-timbered lodge that looks like a fine old Tudor pub, and is as charming as the modern Cripps building is ghastly.

ST JOHN'S *Founded 1511* St John's Street ☺ ☺ ☺ ☺ 🏚 🏚 🏚 🏚

Founded by Lady Margaret Beaufort (her again, see Christ's). This second-largest college crosses the river via the so-called Bridge of Sighs, from which students once hung a car over the river (see page 230).

Much given to roof climbing, a dangerous Cambridge sport. One wag once climbed the New Court tower and painted a clock on one of the stone circles. The master, checking the time, noticed the clock was running slow and sent one of the staff to see if the clock could be fixed. Only when he reached the tower did the man realise that the clock was merely painted on.

St John's contains a curious building, the **School of Pythagoras**, the only large medieval building to survive in Cambridge (most of that era, being timber framed and filled in with wattle and daub or clunch, which is Cambridgeshire clay, have not lasted as well as the stone in this damp, cold climate) and popularly and wrongly claimed to be the oldest part of the university. Eccentrically, this is total balderdash: first, it was not really a school of philosophy at all but a private house and, second, it was the property of an *Oxford* college not a Cambridge one for most of its life. The place, rather severe and church-like given its small windows (Saxon churches were the same, as they could not only not make wide window arches but had little skill with windows, which were often shuttered not glazed) was built as a private house in around 1200. It was bought by Merton College, Oxford, in 1270 and they clearly decided to hang on to it for a year or two ... until 1959, nearly 700 years later, when it was at last transferred to St John's College. Visiting, Chapel, etc – see page 163.

ALUMNI

William Wordsworth, aptly named poet, didn't much like his time at St John's.

William Cecil (1520–98), politician, seems to have been a frightful swot. He arrived at St John's aged only 14 and arranged for the bellringer to wake him at 04.00 every day so he could study in peace. He was to suffer in later life because of the hours he spent in a cramped position at his desk, but by 16 he was lecturing on both Greek and logic. He served as a high adviser to three monarchs – a kind of prime minister although the title had yet to be invented – and became Lord Burghley in 1570.

William Wilberforce (1759–1833) was credited later with helping abolish slave trade, but was a rich dilettante at St John's. (Mind you, when he arrived he was shocked at the goings on. He wrote of 'as licentious a set of men as can well be conceived. They drank hard, and their conversation was even worse than their lives.' Not like now, then.) Wilberforce played cards incessantly and was as free with cutting lectures as he was with cutting the enormous pies he left in his rooms.

Other alumni Prime Ministers **Rockingham** and **Palmerston**; runner **Christopher Brasher** who pretty well invented the London Marathon; *Hitchhiker's Guide to the Galaxy* author **Douglas Adams**; actor **Derek Jacobi**.

FASCINATING FACT The red jackets worn by the college's Lady Margaret Boat Club gave rise to the word 'blazers'.

TRINITY *Founded 1546* Trinity Street ☺ ☺ ☺ ☺ ☺ 🏰 🏰 🏰 🏰 🏰

Trinity College, Trinners to some, while not quite as far up itself as Christ Church, Oxford, is nevertheless pretty damn sure of itself, not without reason, architecturally, academically (31 Nobel prizes, that's more than most entire countries let alone universities) and historically. Oh, and it owns £700 million in properties and cash, and could probably afford to tell the government to get stuffed if it interfered too much.

One of the richest colleges, and certainly the biggest, it was founded at about the same time as Christ Church, in 1546 by Henry VIII, but he took over two older colleges once on this site, King's Hall and Michaelhouse, so it could be said to have an older pedigree. Henry didn't bother to check whether there was already a Cambridge College dedicated to the Trinity – there was, Trinity Hall – so confusion has been caused ever since.

The Great Court quad (the one nearest to Trinity Street) is said to be the biggest in Europe and the alleged setting for a race where students try to run round it before the clock has finished striking 12, as in the film *Chariots of Fire* (see page 30).

ALUMNI

The eccentric Where to start, or finish? **Francis Bacon**, Jacobean politician/philosopher invented frozen food (creating a future opening for one Clarence Birdseye) at the cost of his own life. Bacon, a former Lord Chancellor in the government, was out in a coach with some friends one snowy morning in 1626 when at the top of Highgate Hill in north London he made the coachman stop. He had had a brainwave and wanted to conduct an experiment and, typically, thought there and then the best time for it. He bought a hen from a poor woman in a nearby hovel, disembowelled it, then stuffed the body with snow. He had a strange new idea, laughable to his friends, that freezing could preserve meat.

Unfortunately, it was soon a case of chilled Bacon as much as frozen chicken. He fell ill and was taken to the Earl of Arundel's house nearby. There they put him in a bed but it was damp, having not been not used for a year or so, and Bacon caught pneumonia and soon died. Hence Bacon's Lane next to the cemetery in Highgate, and hence, eventually, a whole new industry for people like Mr Birdseye. There is no record of whether the chicken did, in fact, keep well. But if you pick up a chicken in a freezer marked Best Before End: mid 17th century, that's the one.

One of the less well known eccentric Trinity characters was **William Pugh** who was a fellow in the 1790s. His idea of doing his washing was to throw all his laundry into the River Cam, from which boat users usually retrieved it. It was hung up to dry, whereupon Pugh put the clothes on again. He was given the job of cataloguing the university library but lost it because he read every word in every book, so progress was interminably slow. When he attacked a lamppost in Jesus Lane with a walking stick, accusing it of being Robespierre (the French tyrant), he was judged too bonkers to continue, even at Trinners.

Poets include **George Herbert** and **Andrew Marvell** (whose love poem 'To His Coy Mistress' was as pretty a way of saying 'Phwoar!! Get em off' as one could imagine). Herbert is also described as metaphysical but his purpose was devotional (clutching at a 'rope of sands'). **Byron** (1788–1824) kept a bear, called Bruno or Bruin, in the college, and was famously described as mad, bad, and dangerous to know – the poet, not the bear. He kept the bear as a protest against a rule banning dogs, and thought the bear should teach the fellows manners, and possibly sit examinations. **Dryden;** the Victorian greats **Tennyson** ('Into the valley of Death …'); **Housman** ('those blue remembered hills').

Philosophers include **Bertrand Russell** (so long lived, 1872–1970, whom I recall going to see giving a speech about Ban the Bomb in Trafalgar Square in the 1960s, only later becoming aware that he'd had a completely separate career as an eminent mathematician in the late 19th century!) and **Ludwig Wittgenstein** (If you hope for an intelligent comment, look away now. I do recall a student song which has a rather good line: 'Wittgenstein was a beery swine, who could think you under the table.') who was born at the same time as Adolf Hitler and may have gone to the same school, which frankly must have had a pretty patchy careers advice service. At the other end of his life, as Wittgenstein lay dying, his landlady said to him, as it was his birthday, 'Many happy returns, professor.' He said, dying or not, 'Would you care to rephrase that statement?' Philosophers, eh? In fact, an old Cambridge man tells me of attending a whole year of lectures by a Trinity don on the statement: 'There are no vixens that are not female foxes' and coming to the conclusion that it was true with eight sets of quotation marks.

Politicians The best prime minister we never had, **'Rab' Butler,** chancellor of the exchequer in the 1950s; the first prime minister India ever had, **Jawaharal Nehru,** 1889–1964; three times prime minister **Stanley Baldwin.**

Scientists Endless Nobel prize-winners include **Francis Galton** (1822–1911), the slightly mad explorer/scientist and founder of eugenics (who decided to taste everything in the hospital pharmacy in alphabetical order, and who devised a beauty map of Britain by counting the beautiful women in each town). Unfortunately, his well-publicised eugenics notion, derived from his cousin Charles Darwin's theory of evolution, that you should stop weaker humans breeding and use only the fittest, led eventually to Nazi death camps. He didn't foresee this, but he did discover the anti-cyclone, the use of fingerprints in police work and how to make the perfect cup of tea.

George Airy, the great astronomer, was a smug snob even at primary school; only his brilliance at inventing better peashooters and catapults saved him from his schoolmates. At grammar school, he once repeated 2,394 lines in Latin verse for an examination. He went to Trinity as a sizar in 1819 (which meant he was half student, half servant to save money on fees) but from the start he was teaching others. He graduated as Senior Wrangler (top first-class maths student) in 1823, beat fellow Trinity man **Charles Babbage** (inventor of the first computer, called a calculating engine, which sounds quaint until you remember that we use 'search engines' on the internet) to a professorship and then became Astronomer Royal in 1835. The 1850s see him still arguing with Babbage, this time over broad gauge versus standard gauge for railways, which Airy again won. Responsible for the Airy Transit Circle, a telescope still to be seen at the Royal Observatory, Greenwich, and whose cross hairs define where the world begins and ends.

Isaac Newton invented gravity (well you know what I mean). Although he is remembered for his laws of motion, he was also very interested in the slightly occult art of alchemy, turning lead into gold, dreamed of by medieval scholars. He was a modest man; if you look at the rim of a £2 coin in your pocket you will see his words about how he achieved so much:

Standing on the shoulders of giants

referring to those who went before him. Neither, at the end of his life, did he think he had defined everything, although people wanted to believe he had. He knew someone like Einstein would discover more and said:

I do not know what I seem to the world but to myself, I seem only like a little boy playing on the shore, delighting himself now and then in finding a prettier shell or smoother pebble than ordinary, whilst the great ocean of truth lay undiscovered before me.

You can contemplate a great ocean of beer at the Sir Isaac Newton pub on Castle Hill in his memory.

Royalty Various princes of Wales, some of doubtful intellect and morality, have made Trinity their home in Cambridge. For example, **Prince Albert Victor**, heir to

THE DANGERS OF BEING AN UNDERGRADUATE

Like most universities, Cambridge has always had some eccentric, not to say foolish, student societies. A recent example was the Assassins' Guild which seemed to plot secretly the deaths of just about everyone in the university. When I say secretly, it was in fact on a web page, as follows, with surnames removed in case they have grown up and would, and should, be embarrassed:

- Elizabeth P has a large collection of unusual videotapes, which could become an embarrassment to the Organisation. Dispose of her.
- Paul M has been engaging in unauthorised vigilante activities. The Organisation has requested his termination. Use any methods.
- Matthew H is due for 'early retirement'. Break the news to him. And clean up afterwards.
- Aldabra S has been associating with a notorious psychopath, and has become a threat. Terminate her.
- Austin D has survived being thrown in the Cam, and so is clearly not human. All such mutants must be eradicated.

the future Edward VII when Edward was Prince of Wales. Albert Victor has been accused of being Jack the Ripper (without a lot of evidence, one must say) but

- Jonathan K wishes to leave the Organisation. As you know, there is only one way to leave the Organisation. Send him on his way.
- From: Aldabra S. Mr K should find himself poisoned by a bizarre Creationist leaflet any day now.
- Chris B, notorious hitman for the Trinity Hall mafia, is back in town. Ensure that he stays here. The cemetery would seem a suitable location.
- Angela M has offended people in high places. Escort her to a low place. Six feet under should be sufficient.
- J L has become a security risk, and accordingly will have his privileges removed. Breathing, for a start.
- Ben P is mixing with the wrong sort of people. Ensure that from now on he mixes with nobody. Nobody living, anyway.
- Emil B has leaked vital documents to the Press. Ensure that from now on he leaks only blood.

Clearly they are not given nearly enough work to do. But Aldabra is still a great name …

certainly was by the standards of the day a scandalous pervert. In July 1889 police uncovered the Cleveland Street male brothel scandal. Several high society figures were involved, including Lord Arthur Somerset. The prince's involvement was covered up by perjury, but most of London knew of the rumours. Papers locked away for many years show Somerset saying he told courtiers about the prince's involvement because: 'I thought they ought to know.' He wrote that he had not led the prince to such activities further than 'the fact that we (Prince Eddy and I) must perform bodily functions which we cannot do for each other.' The mind boggles. Luckily, before his father was promoted to king on the death of Queen Victoria, this ungifted putative Prince of Wales died of something tedious.

Other alumni Loads of composers including **Ralph Vaughan Williams** (1872-1958, posh people pronounce the name Raife for the reason that you just can't say Ralph with a plum *and* a silver spoon in your mouth) and to bring things down to earth a little, **A A Milne**, author of *Winnie-the-Pooh*, one of the world's greatest children's books. And if you want to know where he got the ideas for the irrepressible Tigger, the cerebral Owl, and the fatalistic depressive Eeyore, look no further than the students and dons of Cambridge. Christopher Robin, the boy for whom the Winnie-the-Pooh books were written, hated having the book about him in later life; but then at Oxford Alice wasn't particularly interested in the *Wonderland* created for her and as for the boy for whom *Wind in the Willows* was created, well that was just tragic. See *Eccentric Oxford*.

And don't forget, of course, the absolute prince of hoaxers, the hilarious and inimitable **William de Vere Cole** (see page 60).

Then there were two traitors, to be blunt, **Anthony Blunt** and **Guy Burgess**;

FURTHER READING

This College-Studded Marsh by Robert Kenny of Trinity College, 1990. Very enjoyable short book if you can get one, or available at the city library in Lion Yard.

Anthem for Doomed Youth by Jon Stallworthy, Constable 2002. Subtitled *Twelve Soldier Poets of the First World War*, this anthology with commentaries and illustrations is so good that it brings an already powerful subject to vivid reality. Excellent on Cambridge's Rupert Brooke.

Period Piece: A Cambridge Childhood by Gwen Raverat, 1952, reprinted many times. A charming, gentle evocation of a bygone era, recently republished to mark its half century in print. Faber, £9.99, ISBN: 0571067425.

eccentric chocolate heir, test pilot and TV boss **Peter Cadbury**, who died in 2006, and always kept a loaded gun by his bed to deal with burglars (until one of them stole it) and wanted to leave a trust fund for his truculent parrot; *Angel of the North* (or 'Rusty Rita') sculptor **Antony Gormley**; two **Earl Greys** including the tea one, both British/Canadian politicians; novelists **William Makepeace Thackeray** and **Vladimir Nabokov** (who played in goal for Cambridge football team, then wrote *Lolita*); plus a whole list of great historians.

5 More Eccentric Colleges
Other eccentric colleges and the oddballs who have peopled them

Symbols (1–5, the more the merrier)
☺ Eccentric/interesting people
🏰 Architecturally/historically interesting

CHURCHILL *Founded 1960* Storey's Way ☺☺ 🏰

A pair of Churchill students were convicted in 2006 of the extremely rare crime of sending a live hamster through the post. It was said to be revenge by the 19-year-olds on the addressee, or possibly an ill-judged prank, but went down like a lead balloon with the British public, who are always totally appalled by cruelty to dumb animals. The furry dumb chap in Cambridge – the hamster, not the student – had luckily chewed its way out of the envelope and was making its way through a tasty pile of postcards and cheques when the postman found it, otherwise it would have been crushed to death at the sorting office, or at least gone through life with CAMBRIDGE, SEPTEMBER 17, 7PM stamped on its furry forehead.

Press photographers were so outraged at the sheer cruelty to the hamster – now known as First Class – at being heartlessly put in an envelope that they put it back in an envelope to make a good picture. (We know that because the court evidence said the real envelope, cruelly, wasn't padded, but the one pictured in the paper was.) If you carry a knife and stab someone, or kill someone with a car, you can get off with a fine for £200 in this batty country, but in this case the hamster horror duo were punished with the full majesty of the law, and fined £1,450 including costs, and banned from keeping even a goldfish for ten years ('what about stick insects, m'lud?'). Meanwhile Churchill College was forced to put out a disapproving statement vaguely threatening 'what further action is appropriate'. Call me heartless, but *appropriate* further action could include laughing.

Meanwhile you can't be too careful. Post many cards in Cambridge in case hundreds of demented half-starved gerbils are inhabiting the city's pillar boxes.

CLARE HALL *Founded 1965* Herschel Road ☺ 🏰

Not the most original name. Clare Hall was the name for Clare itself for about 500 years, so when that college decided to start a centre for advanced studies, aimed mainly at graduates, it adopted its old name. A non-hierarchical integrated society, apparently, and absolutely brilliant at thinking up amazing new stuff. Except names.

CORPUS CHRISTI *Founded 1352* Trumpington Street ☺ ☺ 🏰 🏰

Once known as Bene't College, because of the church next door. Good college for spies and plague. It is the only college in Oxford and Cambridge set up by the Town, not the Gown. It was founded by the town guilds in 1352 to say masses for the dead after the Black Death which hit England four years earlier. There was a shortage of priests because the pestilence had killed many, thus pushing up mass prices (near mass hysteria), and there were plenty of important dead people, for whom the masses needed to be said. The plague struck Corpus again in the 1630s, when the master of the college, Dr Butts, bravely stayed to tend the dying – corpses at Corpus – and became so unhinged he hanged himself with his garters. He had written in his despair: 'I am alone, a destitute and forsaken man; not a scholar with me in college.' His ghost was said to have been regularly sighted until exorcised in 1904.

Then the college was struck again by the plague in 1665. Only four inhabitants remained while tar and brimstone were kept burning in the gatehouse. So that doesn't work.

As for spies, one of the first must have been the poet **Marlowe** who was recruited here by Queen Elizabeth I's spy chief Walsingham to go to Europe posing as a papist to find out what the exiled Catholics were plotting. He was so convincing in his Catholic role that the university tried to stop his degree, until Walsingham (the James Bond 'M' of his day) had a quiet word. (A quiet word in those days could, of course, be something like: 'Tell me, how would you like to be crushed, stretched until your arms pop out of their sockets, have your entrails torn out in front of you and then be burned?') It was the first of a long and dishonourable tradition of spies being recruited at Cambridge, several of them spying on Britain, such as those high-minded idealists in the 20th century who thought Stalin's Russia was a workers' paradise.

In between those 17th-century plagues, Corpus did indeed show some common sense during the Civil War when the college's plate, that is silverware, was dispersed by the fellows, who were given leave of absence until it was over. Other colleges foolishly sent their treasures to help one side or the other. It was often intercepted by the other side and left the college open to revenge. Meanwhile billeted soldiers would loot anything that remained. Corpus was somewhat cannier.

FASCINATING FACT Long-nosed inquisitive Corpus Master Matthew Parker of 1544 was the original 'Nosey Parker'.

DARWIN *Founded 1964* Silver Street ☺ ▟

About 400 graduate students, half from overseas. Based on a house owned by Charles Darwin – the one who died in 1962, not the famous one, but named after his ancestor, the evolutionary genius. Founded by three older colleges to give graduate studies a boost, and not only backs on to the river but contains two small islands.

Slang name: Emma. History: see page 20. On the college website, the resident ducks get a whole page, with photos.

ALUMNI One has to admire the cheek of Emmanuel undergraduate **Miles Malleson** (1888–1969). He had himself made up to look like a very old MP, William Haddock. He arrived from London on the train, was met by college officials and dined with the master, and later gave an insanely bad lecture opposing votes for women. No-one smelt anything fishy. The lecture was even fully reported by the *Cambridge Daily News*, even though there was no MP called Haddock. Miles Malleson later became a well-known British comedy film actor in the 1930–50s' heyday of Ealing comedies, having roles in *Kind Hearts and Coronets* (he was the affable hangman) and *The Importance of Being Earnest* (he was Canon Chasuble).

Also Monty Python's **Graham Chapman**, who died young in 1989. Fellow Pythoner John Cleese's eulogy was so funny that several other people almost died laughing. It ended: 'Good riddance to bad rubbish, you freeloading bastard', which Chapman would have loved. Actor **Griff Rhys Jones**, playwright **Michael Frayn**, comedian **Graeme Garden**, comedian **Rory McGrath** and **John Harvard** who wasn't a comedian but founded a university at another place, also called Cambridge.

FITZWILLIAM *Founded 1869* Storey's Way ☺ ☺ 🏛

Started in the 19th century as Fitzwilliam Hall, then House, opposite the museum of that name, to give people who could not afford to be in a college a chance to study at Cambridge, but later turned into a college.

ALUMNI Alumni include cricket commentator **Christopher Martin-Jenkins**; TV historian **David Starkey**; Chancellor of the Exchequer **Norman Lamont** and **Subhash Chandra Bose**, the controversial Indian freedom fighter/crypto fascist who thought that a country's freedom (from the British) would come from fighting on the Japanese/Nazi side in World War II; first prime minister and creator of Singapore, **Lee Kuan Yew**. Not so funny as Emmanuel, then.

GIRTON *Founded 1869* Huntingdon Road ☺ ☺ 🏛

The breakthrough for women being allowed into Cambridge University started with the foundation of Hitchin College in 1869 by pioneering educational reformer Emily Davies. It became Girton College in 1872 and moved to Cambridge in 1873.

Now women could go to Cambridge faculty lectures, could live in college, and could sit for examinations, but were not allowed to collect degrees in what seems a petty, mean-spirited restriction. Now admits men too.

ALUMNAE Novelist **Wendy Holden**; **Queen Margrethe II** of Denmark; comedian **Sandi Toksvig** (another great Dane much liked in Britain); and **Princess Takamado** of Japan.

GLOMERY HALL

This school wasn't a college but could have become one. It stood at the corner of what is now the Old Schools, and it was part of the university. It was where the Glomerels studied Glomery – no, I'm not making this up but it does sound Harry Potterish (or the other way round) – which was a corruption of *grammarye* or Latin grammar. It was perhaps a sort of teacher training college of the Middle Ages and indeed the only thing that was taught at such schools was Latin grammar, hence grammar schools. Glomery Hall lasted until around the Reformation in the 16th century. Then Glomery Hall, and the Glomerels, disappeared. A pity, as there was a Master of Glomery, or *Magister Glomeriae*. He was recorded in 1276 as being involved in a dispute between two Glomerels. As usual, it involved the meddling Bishop of Ely.

HOMERTON *Founded 1976* ☺ ♜

Isn't Homerton a place in east London? Yes, and that's where a bunch of Protestant dissenters who had founded the King's Head Society – a sort of semi-underground Congregational Church academy – in 1730, moved their college in 1768. Anyway, after joining the University of London for a bit, it ended up in Cambridge in 1894, became women only, then mixed again, admitted only education students, then any subject. Colleges can wander around like hobos joining different universities and cities at will, this shows. And yesterday's revolutionaries become tomorrow's establishment.

HUGHES HALL *Founded 1885* Mortimer Road ☺ 🏛

The oldest of six graduate colleges, HH opened as Cambridge Training College for Women with just 14 women in a cottage.

LUCY CAVENDISH *Founded 1965* Lady Margaret Road ☺ 🏛

Named after a Queen of Narnia. Or possibly a Victorian campaigner for better women's education. It's about, says the website, enabling women 'to make things happen in their own lives' and nourishing 'the confidence to speak'. Women? Needing the confidence to speak? Are you *kidding?* If that were the case, the mobile phone industry wouldn't be worth gerzillions. But, hasten ye not, ye sexist old gits, for the quote wisely carries on, 'with a voice worth hearing'. Abso-flaming-lutely.

Mind you, speaking out isn't always a totally brilliant idea. A Lucy Cavendish mature student, 45, certainly had the 'confidence to speak' when faced with a jealous wife, 61, who had come to see her about her husband, and attempted to lighten the tone with a jest. The mature student told the ensuing court case in 2006:

'I'm afraid my attempt to lighten the atmosphere before she stabbed me 17 times did not come off.' Evidently.

She added: 'It is very annoying to be stabbed by someone whose husband you're having sex with but doubly annoying to be stabbed by someone whose husband you are not having sex with.' Steamy emails suggested *something* had been going on.

The mature student survived; the wife was jailed for just 30 months (13 months with remand taken into account), the jury having evidently believed her claim that she'd brought the knife with no intention of stabbing anyone except herself and therefore finding her not guilty of attempted murder (but guilty of a lesser charge). Of course, British juries usually see things better than secondhand reports, but I can't help pointing out that at about seven weeks per stab, you'd get a lot longer for not paying your council tax. Or, possibly, parking badly.

NEW HALL *Founded 1954* Huntingdon Road ☺ ⛫

A women's college founded not long after liberalisation (up until which only Girton and Newnham had accepted women). Alumnae include actress **Tilda Swinton** and pulsar discoverer **Joyce Bell Burnell**.

NEWNHAM *Founded 1871* ☺ ☺ ☺ ☺ ⛫ ⛫

Newnham, founded in 1871 to promote excellent education for women (and thus the second women's college after Girton), is known for producing a strange breed known as bluestockings. These are female graduates who become over time doughty dragons, old battleaxes who were once, maybe 50 years previously, pretty undergraduate young gels on a bicycle coming up King's Parade with a wicker front basket stuffed with books.

They are fearless, have been known to face down brigands in remote corners of the Empire, to master and even lead head-hunting tribes and above all to nurture their eccentricities without regard to what anyone else thinks. They can cripple would-be burglars with their umbrellas even in their 90s. They show no undue deference to rank or titles and are often, but not always, the Fabian sort of socialist, independent and radical to their dying days. They often do sterling work for charities – when one of these eccentric old biddies rattles a collecting tin in your face, you dare not refuse.

They waste nothing, using scraps on paper for shopping lists, measuring the right number of cups of water into the kettle as if the war were still on, savings bits of string for God knows what. Of course, not all Newnham alumnae are like that …

ALUMNAE

Pamela, Lady Glenconner (née Paget), born in 1903, was daughter of two eccentric Victorians, a crackpot inventor Sir Richard Paget and batty busybody Lady Muriel Finch-Hatton, who took it upon herself to make it her life's work to rescue English governesses from Russia (even when they didn't want rescuing), as well as helping create Czechoslovakia and run front-line hospitals during World War I (in tsarist

HOW CAMBRIDGE CHANGED THE LIFE OF ONE WOMAN

It was a steamy late-summer evening in 1930 on the steps of a government building in Lahore – after a glittering officers' ball – that my mother, Marjorie Cole, made the astounding decision that would change her life. Marjorie was part of what was mockingly called 'the fishing fleet' – girls of a marriageable age who had left school or college in England and been sent out to India to catch a suitable husband for a lifetime in the service of the Empire. Daughter of the Raj, she had been brought up with plentiful servants; she adored her ayah (maid), was fluent in Hindi and knew the alternative was a life of genteel poverty in freezing England.

My grandmother had sent her to boarding school in Brighton, where she was made to wear shoes that were too small – the result of which was that she had to have a toe amputated. She was not given one minute of science education and there was no coal for the fires in winter. So there she was, a strikingly good-looking, blue-eyed, dark-haired girl of 17, whose whole life had been in preparation for this moment. She was in the company of a rather handsome officer she half-knew who was on one knee on the steps. Good looking, good family, a reasonable income and servants – he might be a decent chap. She looked up at the heavy moon hanging over the city and suddenly said 'No, I'm sorry. I'm going back to England. I'm going to be a doctor.'

'A doctor, but you're a *girl*. You know no science. You need proper Latin, you know,' was the sort of advice she was given, but back in Brighton she first taught herself science and then went to the technical college. She astonished them by winning a place to Newnham College, Cambridge, to read medicine. She qualified, but in the early days women at Oxford and Cambridge weren't permitted to receive the degrees that they had passed. She went into a teaching hospital in London, qualifying just in time for the Blitz. There were many times when people assumed she was the nurse, or asked for a 'man doctor'. She just got on with it.

A few years later, when she was working in Oxford, a brilliant young doctor called Norman Heatley, who became a lifelong friend, gave her a phial of a new medicine to take to a hospital in Banbury where a young girl was dying of infection. It was one of the very first doses of penicillin. The girl was saved.

In the 1950s, after a failed marriage and left with five young boys, she wanted to go back to work but the NHS wouldn't let her because her training was out of date. She worked during the day and re-trained as a psychiatrist at night classes for years and carved out a second career. In retirement, she fought valiantly for victims of mental illness, and helped to set up the National Schizophrenia Fellowship before she died in 1992.

Here I am, years later, with a teenage daughter talking about careers. 'If only your grandmother were here,' I say. 'She'd have told you, "You can do *anything*."'

That's the difference the opening of Cambridge made to women.

Russia, naturally). Asked about news of Lady Paget's extraordinary exploits and whether they were related, Sir Richard was wont to say evasively, although truthfully: 'Only by marriage.'

Sir Richard's mad experiments included filling his daughters' ears with treacle, inventing a sign language and getting young Pamela to throw herself backwards off a London bus, when it was running at 35mph down Park Lane, because he theorised that the air current would make her land on her feet. She did, and survived to marry Lord Glenconner in 1925 after reading English at Newnham. The bridesmaids were dressed in lurid colours of stained glass, and the groom's brother, the notorious 'Bright Young Thing' and louche Stephen Tennant (an eccentric aristocrat who spent most of his life in bed), brought a snake and a tortoise as guests in his pockets, much to the hysterical reaction of the bridesmaids. Pamela divorced in 1935 and became

fearsomely involved in various London charities and causes, later joining a sit-in of protesting students in the 1960s at a college of which she was a governor. She lived in Campden Hill, near Kensington, after 1949 and had a famously miserable bearded housemaid, who once opened the door to two members of the royal family coming to a lunch party and said grumpily: 'Two *more!*' Pamela, Lady G, died in 1989.

Marietta Pallis (1882–1963) was an eccentric and mysterious blend of botanist (in fact ecologist before that idea had been invented) and enthusiast for all things Greek. But then she was something of a strange blend herself, having been born in India of Greek parents, educated in England before going up to then new Newnham College. Pallis in her work with the Central Committee for the Survey and Study of British Vegetation and the Royal Geographical Society before and during World War I helped to evolve what is now known as the ecology idea: that plants can't be taken in isolation but are part of a system. She moved increasingly into pursuits such as art (painting in particular), travel and the celebration of Greek culture and Greek Orthodoxy, which she felt were threatened by the modern and dominant Western world – and the terrible wars that raged across Europe twice in her lifetime. I have had fleeting glimpses of this interesting woman's life without really grasping the whole story. Somewhere I once read, and can't find again, that she discovered and studied a floating island system in the Danube, and worked to protect them by pointing out they were dependent on developments hundreds of miles away up river in different countries. These islands – more accurately fens – are a sort of thatch of vegetation big enough to live on, or at least land on, floating in a delta. Sounds rather *Gulliver's Travels*ish.

What is certain is that she spent the last part of her life living near Hickling Broad in Norfolk. This is the largest and loneliest of these waterways, a wonderful place for a boat trip, with little between you and Norway except cold sea. A very strange, eerie and to my mind utterly beautiful place, where the vast lake surrounded by reeds and bogs stands only a short walk from the North Sea (particularly from the Horsey Mere branch of the waterway) yet flows away from it and is in fact about 20 miles away from its connection with the sea at Yarmouth. Here she studied peat (as one does) and was part of the stunning discovery, surprisingly recently, that the Norfolk Broads system of linked lakes aren't natural at all but are flooded remains of forgotten medieval peat diggings (one of the leading figures in this was Joyce Lambert, a Newnham researcher and friend of Pallis). Amazing. Like suddenly finding out the Isle of Wight was put there by the Romans. She managed to link her love of Greek and peat (how many people boast that particular duo of passions I don't know) by excavating a truly bizarre pool, making an island in the shape of a double-headed Byzantine eagle at her home at Long Gores Marsh and, some say, frequently swimming around it. It has two Greek letters in the base of it which look to me on an aerial photo like those for MP – her initials. She died in 1963 and was buried on the island along with her companion, one Phyllis Clarke (or Riddle as one source has it, which seems to have been a maiden name). Riddle or not, you may suppose that after 40 years the two of them may now be part of her beloved peat. Alternatively, as other discoveries in East Anglia have shown, peat is a pretty good preservative, not to say possibly perfect pickler, of the human corpse over a dozen centuries. May they rest in peat.

Other alumnae MP **Diane Abbott**; actresses **Eleanor Bron** and **Emma Thompson**; jockey/sports presenter **Clare Balding**; feminist **Germaine Greer** (a doctorate); TV presenter **Joan 'Thinking man's crumpet' Bakewell**; novelists **Margaret Drabble**, **A S Byatt** and **Iris Murdoch**.

PEMBROKE *Founded 1347* Pembroke Street ☺ ☺ ☺ 🏛 🏛 🏛

Called by some Pem or Pemmers. Some upper-class twits, that is. Founded by the French-born Countess of Pembroke as a consolation after her husband died in a joust on their wedding day, or less romantically from overeating (apoplexy and terminal flatulence on rising from the table, à la *Grande Bouffe*). Scholars were barred from 'drunkenness, taverns, contentiousness, lechery and notable viciousness' in perpetuity, so report any you see breaking these rules. Preference was to be given to Frenchmen, and French was to be spoken when Latin was not, although whether they found any Frenchmen ready to disdain alcohol and lechery we don't know.

Roger Long, Master of Pembroke from 1733 to 1770, used to ride a homemade watercycle around the pond in the college gardens. He was appointed professor of modern history in 1768 although he knew nothing at all about it, which he admitted, and never gave a lecture. But he at least invented the pedalo, and, arguably, the planetarium, one of which he built, a sort of globe with room for 30 people to sit inside it and watch the heavens rotate about them.

A student prankster must have been thinking of Roger Long on 29 May 1822 when notices went up around Cambridge saying: 'Zachariah Whitmore, of Philadelphia, North America, begs to inform the inhabitants of Cambridge that he intends starting from Lynn on his Water Velocipede at 12 o'clock, and will arrive at Cambridge between 6 and 7 o'clock in the evening on Whit Monday next.' Two thousand people lined the river bank, no doubt watched by the hoaxer, but no such machine turned up. Zachariah Whitmore, indeed!

ALUMNI include **William Pitt The Younger** who became Prime Minister at the age of only 25; comedian/actors **Tim Brooke-Taylor, Peter Cook, Eric Idle, Bill Oddie**; Australian writers **Clive James**, **Tom Sharpe**; actor **Bernard Miles**; poets **Thomas Gray** and **Ted Hughes**.

PETERHOUSE *Founded 1284* Trumpington Street ☺ ☺ ☺ ☺ ♜ ♜ ♜

ALUMNI Among the more interesting Petreans are:

Arts Musician **Colin Greenwood**, bass player for the 1990s band Radiohead; **Richard Baker**, the avuncular television newsreader of the 1960–80s; actor **James Mason**, one of those Brits with a darker side Hollywood absolutely loved in the 1940–70s; plus

Sam Mendes, film director/producer/Mr Kate Winslet; poets **Richard Crashaw** and **Thomas Gray**. (Yes, the latter should be listed under Pembroke too. He was obsessed with the dangers of dying in a fire, and made his own escape ladder. When pranksters made one false alarm too many, he decamped to Pembroke.)

Science Inventor of the hovercraft **Christopher Cockerell** (see page 65); **Frank Whittle** who in the 1930s invented the jet engine (and was ignored by officialdom as usual, until it was too late to affect World War II); **Charles Babbage** who invented the computer – a mechanical version called a Difference Engine – in the early 19th century; he'd moved from Trinity. Then there was eccentric 18th-century scientist **Henry Cavendish**, who wore a three-cornered hat, an outdated crumpled velvet suit and frilled short cuffs and discovered nitric acid and hydrogen (which he called 'inflammable air'). Both of his grandfathers were dukes. At the end of his life he told his servant to take a message because he was about to die, and then did.

Also Nobel Prize winners **Sir Aaron Klug**, **Archer Martin** and **Max Poerutz**. Most whole universities round the world would like to have *one* Nobel Prize winner, so this should not be underestimated.

Politics Prime Minister the **Duke of Grafton** (PM 1768–70). Also would-be-prime-minister **Michael Howard**, who was Home Secretary and later leader of the Conservative Party in opposition. Famously asked the same question many times by Jeremy Paxman (see page 129). Howard, who had some connection with the homeland of the fictional Count Dracula, was described by Ann Widdecombe as 'having something of the night about him' (and they were on the same side!). Unfairly regarded as a failure as Tory leader because he lost the 2005 election whereas in fact more people in England voted Conservative than Labour (who won only because of Scottish and Welsh seats and a general bias in constituency boundaries), so he can't have done that badly. Plus another top Tory, **Michael Portillo**. They were both children of refugees, which made the Tory focus on immigration in the 2005 election an interesting choice.

ROBINSON *Founded 1979* Grange Road ☺ 🏰

ALUMNI Lyricist **Charles Hart** must be worth a few bob as he wrote the words for *Phantom of the Opera*; sculptor **Marc Quinn** who made Alison Lapper famous by putting her naked and pregnant on a pedestal in Trafalgar Square. You see, girls, some day your plinth will come.

ST CATHARINE'S *Founded 1473* ☺ ☺ 🏰 🏰

Rebuilt in the 17th century. The master in the 1660s was John Eachard who had the task of examining the young Isaac Newton for his BA in 1665. Eachard had the temerity to attack the use of Latin to study just about anything in 1670, which brought down a heap of insults on his head. He was called 'a rebel, traytor, Scot, sadducee and Socinian, Barbarian, Indian, Turk and Jew.' Whatever his denigrators studied, it was clearly neither rhetoric, nor indeed logic. How could anyone be all these things at once?

Slang name: Cats or Catz.

ALUMNI TV inquisitor **Jeremy Paxman**, who famously asked former Home Secretary Michael Howard the same question 12 times in May 1997. It is fascinating, appalling and hilarious to watch as Howard avoids answering it again and again. It's one of the most popular bits of video on the BBC website. Paxo, as the tabloid newspapers like to call him because it's a brand of stuffing and annoys him, comes over as a relentless intellect making no compromises, which is why he was selected to chair *University Challenge*, a varsity quiz show revived in the 1990s. He once looked deeply pained as a mere Portsmouth undergraduate said: 'Sorry, don't know, mate.' Scornfully, Paxo retorted, 'That's all right, *mate*.'

Also **John Addenbrooke** who founded the hospital; theatre director **Peter Hall**; *Chocolat* author **Joanne Harris**; *Under the Volcano* author **Malcolm Lowry;** first Malaysian prime minister **Tunku Abdul Rahman.**

SAINT EDMUND'S *Founded 1896* ☺ 🏰

Not named after a Prince of Narnia. Originally for the first Roman Catholics allowed into Cambridge. A graduate college.

SELWYN *Founded 1882* Grange Road ☺ ☺ 🏛

The college was founded in 1882 with the Anglican Church very much its focus.

Bishops aren't supposed to do silly stuff like pranks, are they? George Augustus Selwyn, born 1809, after whom Selwyn College was named, became the first Bishop of New Zealand. When he was a young man he was visiting Heidelberg in what was to become Germany when he took to using the students' swimming pool. This was of the sort fed through a pipe from a river, to which the water returned via another pipe. I remember one of these at Oxford. You could be breast-stroking away and come face-to-face with a pike. Or something worse. Selwyn dived into the German pool and disappeared from view in the somewhat murky waters. After five minutes, panic ensued and students sent for helpers to find the body. Then a grinning Selwyn resurfaced – he had swum through the pipe into the river and surfaced there before returning the way he had come. Holy mackerel!

ALUMNI TV's **Malcolm Muggeridge** and **Clive Anderson**, **Hugh 'House MD' Laurie**; novelist **Richard Harris**; politicians **John 'burgermeister' Gummer** and **Simon Hughes**; scientist **Simon LeVay** who discovered that gay brains are different to straight people's brains.

SIDNEY SUSSEX *Founded 1596* Sidney Street ☺ ☺ 🏛 🏛

Set up with the help of bribery, Sidney Sussex has produced spies, murderers and a tyrant (whose much-mangled remains it still protects), has been associated with violence from time to time, has endured poverty and even had students eating donkey.

But that's to concentrate unfairly on the positive.

No, no, joke, sorry, *negative*, definitely. Despite having endured a bad press for centuries – mainly through its association with intolerant, ruthless victor of the Civil War **Oliver Cromwell** – Sidney Sussex has emerged in the last century or so as a haven of academic excellence and the producer of some decent human beings.

Cromwell isn't, of course, a villain to some, as his statue outside the House of Commons at Westminster shows. He established the supremacy of that chamber above all else, and finally established that kings and their corrupt élite couldn't tax and spend without asking Parliament. It was a 'no taxation without representation' lesson hard-learned – by Charles I having his head distanced from his body with an axe in 1649. If only that had been applied to our American chums in the following century, they would now be playing cricket, drinking tea and morris dancing (a narrow escape for them, they may think). What concerns us here is Cromwell's time at Sidney Sussex, and his strange return. At the restoration of the monarchy in 1660, royalists dug up the body of Cromwell (and many of his henchmen).

True to nearly all revolutions, they had become as bad as tyrants as those they'd replaced, and went round burning supposed witches, mistreating prisoners, executing enemies, smashing stained glass, including here in Cambridge, beheading statues, banning books and closing theatres. Not unlike certain religious fundamentalists today, they were less about fun or fundament and more about mental.

Just as in Mao's China and Robespierre's France, a lot of people thought the *ancien régime* can't have been that bad after all, and so brought Charles II to the throne.

Cromwell, who had died in the meantime, was dug up and decapitated. His head was exhibited on a spike for 25 years, after which – although the custom was to parboil such heads of traitors to give them a fresh and ruddy appearance – it was way past its 'best before' date.

It then was removed, buried, dug up again, used as a football, buried again etc until 1960, when the now-three-centuries-old head was acquired by its former college and buried in Sidney Sussex grounds. Given that monarchists still want to dig Cromwell's head up and further mistreat it, the grave was unmarked and its precise location is known to only a few people. Come to think of it, it could be a rather good fund-raiser: get a square yard of Sidney Sussex grounds for £100, and if you pick the one with the rotted head in it you win ...

In the 19th century the college clearly needed fund-raisers. One of the fellows bought a donkey, and fattened him up on oats (the origin of the story of donkey oaty, possibly?), then the dining hall ate every part of him which tasted 'delicious, rather like swan'. Which for most people is as helpful as saying the flesh of a centaur tastes rather like that of a unicorn. Anyway, one Eeyore-like depressive pointed out that the stench of the fat in the kitchens was disgusting, so much so that the man who collected it weekly (for what purpose?) refused to do so and it had to be buried at some distance. So do us all a favour and don't dig near Sidney Sussex, lest you unearth a rotted head and oodles of vile donkey fat.

ALUMNI TV cleverclogs **Carol Vorderman** (who appeared on *Countdown* with Richard Whiteley, see page 71); 1970s politician David, later **Lord Owen**.

TRINITY HALL *Founded 1350* Trinity Lane ☺ ☺ ☺ 🏰 🏰 🏰

Like actress **Rachel Weisz**, one of its more recent alumnae, Trinity Hall is not too large, not as proud as better-known rivals, but very pretty. Didn't Henry James say: 'If I were called upon to mention the prettiest corner of the world, I should draw a thoughtful sigh and point the way to the gardens of Trinity Hall'?

Why 'Hall'? Actually most of the 14th-century foundations were Halls, not Colleges, having developed from more informal hostels for scholars. Properly the Hall of the Holy Trinity of Norwich. Most have dropped the Hall name, but it is retained here to differentiate it from Trinity which Henry VIII thoughtlessly plonked down near by. Founded by Bishop Bateman of Norwich in 1350 to help cope with the shortage of lawyers caused by the Black Death, (not all bad news, then, plague). Bateman did a lot for Cambridge and is remembered in the street named after him.

In Elizabethan times the college achieved another milestone in its history – well, several literally. It took upon itself the task of repairing the road to London, which is why on the A10 such as between Royston and Cambridge you often see milestones with Trinity Hall arms upon them. Gabriel Harvey, one of Trinity Hall's masters was supervising road building at around that time when he was mocked by a passing nobleman: 'Doctor, you think this causeway is the high road to Heaven.' Harvey retorted: 'Not so, sir, for then I think I should not have met you in this place.'

A neat riposte, for it is unwise to make smart comments to an Oxbridge academic who may be smarter than yourself. I am reminded of Oxford's founder of Methodism, John Wesley. When he met Beau Nash, the elegant dandy of Jesus College, on a narrow pavement, Nash said arrogantly: 'I never give way for a fool.' Wesley, being a Christian, stepped into the muddy street, saying: 'I always do.'

FAVOURITE ECCENTRIC MASTER Henry Latham who ruled from 1888 to 1902. He had a speech problem, not being able to say his Rs clearly. He told recent arrivals at the college: 'You must either wead, wide or wow.' A bit like having Wadio 2 DJ Jonathan Woss as your mentor. Wossie won't mind our mentioning his speech problem, if it is one, as he's made a caweer of it. Latham also couldn't tell one woman from another, he said, 'because they are all so much alike'. Wossie seems to be more clued up on that subject.

In fact, the 'wolled r' first came to notice as an upper-class affectation (and I wouldn't dream of accusing Wossie of that), being popular in the fashionable set of Georgiana, Duchess of Devonshire in the late 18th century. It was part of a drawl, or indeed dwawl, whereby yellow became 'yaller' and various lisps adopted. Thackeray even notes the 'armah' unit pronounced as the 'Heavy Cawalwy' and by the mid 19th century there were upper-class types who had not so much a silver spoon in their mouths as a whole canteen with soup spoons, ladles, cruet set, candlesticks and a sack of plums too. Lady Caroline Lamb was almost incomprehensible to normal people, for example. Perhaps they thought it cute – not so very elevated above American cartoons going on about a 'pesky wabbit', is it?

Slang name 'Tit Hall'.

ALUMNI The aforementioned actress **Rachel Weisz** (London-born daughter of a Hungarian inventor; films include *Enemy at the Gates, The Mummy, About a Boy*); comedian **Tony Slattery** (films include *The Wedding Tackle, To Die For)*; Buddhist high court judge **Christmas Humphreys**; movie/stage director **Nicholas Hytner**.

Also mild-mannered former chancellor of the exchequer **Lord (Geoffrey) Howe.** His predecessor Denis Healey memorably described being attacked by

Howe as like 'being savaged by a dead sheep'. His wife Elspeth, in recognition of his having been made a knight, then a peer, then herself being made a peer, is sometimes jokingly called Lady Lady Lady Howe, three times a lady.

Former Archbishop of Canterbury **Lord Runcie** eccentrically preferred his pigs to politicians any day, which made him rather like Lord Emsworth in those Jeeves books. Runcie once said: 'I wish I could turn my attention to such things as tranquil as my Berkshires.'

Going back further, one **Henry Fawcett**, who was blinded by his father's gun at a shooting party, but turned out to be one of the bravest, most successful and charitable men this college has ever produced (page 52).

Going back a lot further, Elizabethan politician **Lord Howard**, and poet **Robert Herrick** (1591–1674) who wrote memorably:

Gather ye rosebuds while ye may,
Old Time is still a-flying:
And this same flower that smiles to-day,
To-morrow will be dying.

Which is after all only saying, albeit rather prettily, phwoar, get yer kit off. Less successful, you may feel, is his line:

Fain would I kiss my Julia's dainty leg,
Which is as white and hairless as an egg.

OK, legs and eggs rhyme, but have you met a woman who was content to be compared with such a lowly, everyday thing? Julia would have slapped him for mentioning that there might conceivably have been hair. 'Don't you know women are sensitive about such things? Why mention hair *at all*, then if you're so pleased with me? Do you *know* how *humiliated* I was?' Poem thrown in fire, exit right with slammed door and intention to spend all Herrick's 72 groats on needless shopping for these so-cool expensive trendy New World imports, potatoes and tobacco. She knows you boil one and set fire to the other, although which was which …

WOLFSON *Founded 1965* Barton Road ☺ 🏰

A graduate college, as is the same-named one at Oxford.

HUMMING HEADLINE

Churchill College is – despite being home to a predominantly sciencey crowd – a bastion of student journalism, in the usual subversive, not to say doubtful, undergraduate taste displayed in their magazine *Winston*. Headline in late 1997: Did diddy dodgy Dodi do dear dead Di?

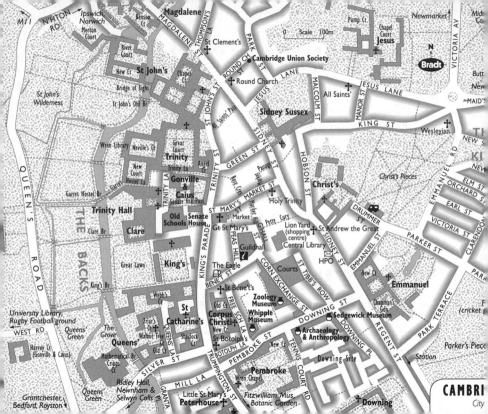

6 Eccentric Living

Eat, drink, stay and shop eccentric

EAT ECCENTRIC

SWISH

Midsummer House Restaurant Overlooking Midsummer Common; ☎ 01223 369299

Difficult to get to without instruction. By car: proceed around ring road to Chesterton Road, turn into Ferry Path, turn left as you have to into De Freville Avenue, turn right into Hamilton Road then into Pretoria Road where you park. Walk to footbridge at the end of Pretoria Road, cross River Cam. Restaurant is on the left. Once owned by TV celeb Chris Kelly, somebody told me breathlessly. If true, so what? Who is he? Is the food any good? Well, yes. In a Victorian villa beside the Cam. Cuisine: French Mediterranean. *Typical three courses: £55 per head.*

GOOD VALUE AND EXPENSIVE

Fitzbillies Trumpington St; ☎ 01223 352500

If you can afford it, highly recommended. Bloody marvellous, as it transpires. This is perfectly cooked and presented food served by staff who are unfussy in suitably unfussy but relaxing surroundings yet interested and polite (unlike those cretins who come round singing 'is everything all right?' every five minutes in places that clearly aren't and never will be). As an expensive experiment we ordered three of their fillet steaks, one well done, one medium, and one medium rare. They were all perfectly cooked to their different standards and having tried all three (vegetarians who don't want to know the result look away now) it was an education. I will never, ever waste expensive and beautiful cuts of beef by having them well done again. Compared to the other two, it could have been a cheaper cut, for all the subtlety that was left, and that was entirely the fault of the customer not the chef. Hence the bloody marvellous.

This place is somehow connected to the fabulous Fitzbillies bakery next door, with its friendly bun-like lettering familiar from years ago (cripes, I say Bunter, iced buns for tea!). The name surely comes from the Fitzwilliam Museum across the road, or the eponymous college. As for price at the restaurant, well we did go a bit mad. Four starters (all very good), two smoothies, three fillet steaks, two lattes, two bottles of their own Aussie red (which was not a house plonk, but frankly as fine a wine as you'll find this side of £25 for half the price), more Aussie red (well it was that good and that kind of night), no room for puddings, and the bill came to £97.25. OK, OK, yes I know it's a lot, but trust me, after all that excellent wine it doesn't hurt and it's only plastic.

Anyway, if you and your chums did without cheap deep-fried pub grub for a couple of days, it would work out at the same cost and you'd be happier, healthier and wiser. Even if one or more of your party were to die of hunger while saving up, it would still be worth it. It's not a huge place and unpretentious, so you might want to book. Try not to fall into the gutters of Trumpington Street (wider and deeper than usual) as you (also wider and deeper) sway happily home.

GOOD VALUE AND MEDIUM
No 1 King's Parade ☏ 01223 359506
As opposed to the somewhat canteen-like Copper Kettle a few doors down (which copes valiantly with truckloads of tourists), this is altogether more elegant and offers creatively cooked and carefully presented

fare, still at affordable — but not rock-bottom — prices. For such a touristy spot, it's surprisingly attentive and good value. There are often lunchtime specials (at time of my visit summer vegetable soup with crusty French bread £4.35; traditional fish and chips including a glass of wine £6). Light lunch for three (puddings but no booze) cost us £33.50. You can spend a lot more on a lot worse. We ate in the airy upstairs (ground floor, shop level that is) to watch the Japanese tourists, various Cambridge nutters, cycling students, protesting politicos and doolally dons wander past, but there's a restaurant downstairs for more of an à la carte style.

Hobb's Pavilion Parker's Piece ✆ 01223 367480
In an old cricket pavilion and a tribute to cricket legend Jack Hobbs who played here. Mediterranean-style food and plenty of open space to gaze upon, only a short stroll from central Cambridge. Cricket-related guff on display.

Varsity Restaurant 35 St Andrew's St; ✆ 01223 356060.
This place has been doing reliable, interesting, fair-priced Cypriot food for more than 50 years. I couldn't believe it was still there. The Whim, if you remember that and are rediscovering a misspent youth, really isn't there any more, thank God. Well, whim some, lose some.

GOOD VALUE AND CHEAP AS CHIPS
The Gardenia Rose Crescent
This cheap and cheerful almost greasy spoon Greek takeaway is included purely out of sentiment, for it's just as it was 40 years ago when impoverished students would gather there after a night out. Little known

is that you can eat in by going upstairs to a cosy dining room which, like the fish, is somewhat battered but a refuge from the hubbub below. Next to this, artfully concealed for once, is McDonald's, with whom this successfully competes.

TEA ROOMS AND CAFÉS

Clown's King St

A nice place to hang out slightly away from the tourist hubbub. Copy of *The Guardian* and a beard almost de rigueur.

Trockel Ulmann und Freunde Pembroke St

A very small, cosy place. You perch on high stools like in a chemistry lab, but worth it for good coffee, excellent soup (which seems to be mainly vegetarian) and fresh bread.

The Michael House Café Old St Michael's Church, Trinity St

Light, pleasant atmosphere in a redundant church if you don't mind the odd eccentricity like gravestones in the gents. Many people think European cities have too many churches because the population has (a) fled, or (b) become irreligious, Muslim or something. Actually there always were too many — they just liked building them as acts of faith and insurance policies by being nice to the relevant saint.

Fitzbillies Trumpington St

The best belt-loosening Chelsea buns this side of, well, the asteroid belt (and possibly beyond). Not very eccentric, but very comfortable, as the lettering above the shop implies.

Auntie's Tea Shop Opposite Great St Mary's between King's Parade and the market; ✆ 01223 315641
Traditional cream teas and cakes on fancy plates, plus light lunches. Not even faintly eccentric.

DRINK ECCENTRIC

The Pickerel Inn Magdalene St; ✆ 01223 355068
Aren't they those things you have millions of in digital cameras? No, it's a fish, appropriately enough as it's just over the river on the left, going over Magdalene Bridge away from the city centre. The Americans have a pickerel fish too, whom I've never met, but here it is the young of the pike, a vicious, bony fish that just loves East Anglian waterways. Said to be the oldest pub in Cambridge and once a brothel and an opium den. Low beams, bags of atmosphere, small, good quality but inexpensive food (no pickerel sandwiches though), not particularly aimed at children but there is a yard out the back with tables if the weather is warm enough.

The Eagle Bene't St (very central, off King's Parade going towards the Guildhall)
For fame, atmosphere, history and good beer this takes a lot of beating. As I say elsewhere, the plaque on the front tells that this is where the secret of life, DNA, was first unravelled by Crick & Watson (well, they did it in the laboratory, but announced it here). And no it wasn't one of those nights where you tell your friend: 'You're so brilliant mate, I really, really, love you,' in a slurred voice as you cling to them for support. They were brilliant, and they had discovered life's hidden double helix. They got the idea from the double spiral staircase in the pub. No they didn't – that was a complete fib. But they should install one in their honour.

The high entrance to the yard shows this, the former Eagle and Child, was once a coaching inn. Its mullioned windows show its age, and it was the headquarters of a notorious swindler in the 18th century.

But the best is yet to come — go to the back bar and look at the strange ceiling decoration: weird patterns in black and red on a reddish base. These are the signatures of hard-drinking fast-living airmen who peopled the British and American air bases of East Anglia's 'unsinkable aircraft carrier' in World War II. The young men — 19 or 20, some of them — stood on the tables and used their cigarette lighters to draw their initials, the names of their squadrons, outlines of pin-up girls. Several of those who left a mark here climbed into their cockpits and took off into the big East Anglian skies and never made it home. If ever graffiti deserved respect, it is here, and thank God no-one painted it over, you may think as you sup a pint. There's the story about just one chap who didn't make it back alive to the Eagle on the wall.

Appropriately, for the soaring young Americans who flew from bases near here, the Eagle is their national symbol as well as the name of the pub.

The St Radegund King St

This pub conceals a strange secret under its floor — an ancient holy well. King Street is also famed for the King Street Run where students would take a pint of ale at each pub in that short street — the number of pubs has varied but was nine at one point. At least it's survivable, unlike the Rose Street ramble in Edinburgh where around 20 pubs need to be visited. And, oh yes, it should be done within an hour. See King Street walk, page 169.

King Street Run King St

The former Horse and Groom, named after the above-mentioned pub crawl, is deeply eccentric. All the doors you should push have PULL signs on and vice versa. A sane person pointed this out to me because I invariably do the wrong one and did so here too. There are large holes in the ceiling so you can see the upstairs bar from downstairs. It all has something of a mad junkyard atmosphere, with corrugated iron on the ceiling. The upstairs balustrade is formed of things like chairlegs and mops and is hopelessly crooked. A shelf laden with tins and jars is fixed upside down, defying Isaac Newton's laws. Everything is crooked — except the landlord and the pool table. And the real ale is acceptably flat too. Has to be seen to be disbelieved.

Champion of the Thames King St

The complete opposite to the above. Wacky brashness replaced by a pub of real elegance, beauty and perfection. And that's just the outside. The name, frankly, is the triumph of hope over experience as far as the Boat Race is concerned, an agent of Another Place told me as we nevertheless enjoyed a good pint. Can be crowded sometimes, so get there early for a seat or be prepared to row through the throng.

The Free Press Prospect Row off Warkworth St (best described as behind the police station on Parker's Piece, a large green open space on the way to the station; you reach it by Warkworth Terrace off Parkside, on the park side as it happens)

The antidote to tourist-thronged pubs such as the Eagle (above). Quiet and unassuming, partly because it's off the beaten track and you wouldn't go there unless you were going there.

As a journalist, I was interested whether the name was a tribute to the glories of a free press, and was hugely amused to find it was an attack on it.

Just as local woman Sarah Horne first opened her cottage here to the public to sell her home brew in 1834, the temperance (teetotal) movement launched a paper called *The Free Press* to campaign against the dangers of drinking. She named her pub after their paper in ironic mockery. The paper lasted but one issue, the pub nearly two centuries. Puritan Prodnoses 1, Demon Drink 172 (game still in progress).

While real alcoholism is a ghastly thing, an England without pubs would be pretty ghastly too. And where better to celebrate that than The Free Press with its great food and excellent ale? The tiny snug bar, by the way, once held 59 Downing students. Small ones, evidently.

Ancient Druids Napier St off Newmarket Rd (at the back of the same block of streets as The Free Press)
Its name is one of those titles like Holy Roman Empire which is not entirely accurate, being neither Ancient nor Druid. It certainly isn't the Ancient Druids I recall when a student at the nearby Tech, that pub having been knocked down to build the Grafton Centre. Not that it doesn't do good beer and food. Just no chanting weirdos in white robes (well, not on Tuesdays when I was there).

The Regal Regent St
I have heard beer bores and pub snobs sneer at this former-cinema-turned-beer-and-food-hall — perhaps because it is part of a more successful chain than anything they could ever devise, or maybe because of the sheer scale of it which is almost industrial. No doubt cinema nuts could object too. I love the pubs and beers of old England as much as any man, but also appreciate the pretty well unspoilt interior of a sumptuous 1930s Art Deco cinema which has, miraculously, been more or less preserved. It has the atmosphere of a great ocean liner of the day, and as for its size, that's an asset because you can find your own table and have space and privacy for whatever tryst you have in mind, unlike some shoebox Cambridge pubs I can think of. The food is inexpensive, fast and safely unsurprising, which is after all what most people want if they are not feeling adventurous. A city like Cambridge needs all kinds of pubs and it's hardly the fault of the pub that people after the last war bought televisions, and later videos and DVDs, so giant picture palaces were no longer needed. Wetherspoons and other new users elsewhere are merely

picking up the pieces. There is in fact an Arts Cinema upstairs here, strangely divorced from the grand entrance downstairs.

Built in 1937 as the 'ultimate in comfort and convenience', the Regal's first feature was *Swing Time* with Fred Astaire and Ginger Rogers. Cheap seats were 6d and posh ones half a crown (2s 6d, or 12 and a half pence in new money). For the sake of those who don't remember, for that money in the following couple of decades you would have got a newsreel (when everyone went to the cinema and nobody had a television it was the main source of news footage, in black and white of course, with that corny stirring commentary) and maybe a B movie (a short feature) before the main picture. At the very end you had to stand for the national anthem to be played, so a lot of people rushed for the doors while the credits were rolling ...

The Cabinet Reed (a tiny village near Royston on the A10 heading back towards London); ☏ 01763 848366 Worth including because it's so quiet, so special and so hidden away. The food in the award-winning restaurant is largely good local produce, the beer excellent. The locals try to keep this place secret. Take the turning on the left marked Reed a couple of miles south of Royston and it's in the High Street (but it's really in the middle of nowhere).

GAY PUBS The **Fleur de Lys** in Humberstone Road and the **Bird in Hand** in Newmarket Road were said to be popular with gay people at the time of writing. Not exclusively so, however.

RIVERSIDE PUBS The **Mill** in Mill Lane (☏ *01223 357026*) and the **Anchor** (☏ *01223 353554*) down parallel Silver Street, are good and busy on a hot day when customers of the former spill outside and across the river, given plastic glasses so they can enjoy the outside (and not the very hot and rather small interior on such days). If you want to sit down, the Anchor has more interior room and better places to sit and see people pratting about in punts. There aren't that many pubs on the river, because the colleges own the Backs from here to beyond Magdalene Bridge. But on the open spaces down river from there are some more. The **Fort St George** (↘ *01223 354327*) on Midsummer Common has a splendid site and lots more room.

The world's rudest publican: see page 48.

STAY ECCENTRIC

For a full list see the tourist information office (page 153) but here is a selection with 2006 published rates, cheapest last.

Hotel Felix Whitehouse La, Huntingdon Rd; ↘ 01223 277977; www.hotelfelix.co.uk
Cool, designer, chic, a work of art. If these kind of words, used on their website, float your boat, and you can afford it. Not too convenient for the city centre or railway station, given the price, but no doubt relentlessly cool. *At time of writing from £168 inc b/fast, or from £350 for 2 nights inc b/fasts and £30 pp towards a meal in their restaurant, Graffiti (drinks exc).*

Arundel House Hotel Chesterton Rd; ☎ 01223 367701; f 01223 367721;
e info@arundelhousehotels.co.uk; www.arundelhousehotels.co.uk

Nice site overlooking the Cam and Jesus Green open space (and the busy Chesterton Rd). Walkable to the city centre. Restaurant and also colonial-style conservatory brasserie with a ficus benjamina tree in the middle of it. They also own the nearby Ashley Hotel, so may offer to divert you there if full. *Sgl from £75, dbl £95–120.*

The Lensfield Hotel 53 Lensfield Rd; ☎ 01223 355017; www.lensfieldhotel.co.uk

This is well-sited, Lensfield Rd being on the right as you approach by car from London off the M11 and up Trumpington Rd, or on the left on the Hills Rd route from the railway station, and offering a short stroll up Trumpington St to the city centre. However, it is not a regular hotel, according to the AA, but rated as 'guest accommodation', being a series of houses on this street that have been knocked together. It has been run by the same Greek Cypriot family since it opened more than four decades ago, and while it isn't quite like walking into My Big Fat Greek Wedding, there were plenty of friendly family members around on our visit. Our room was spacious, the beds comfortable but there aren't a lot of other facilities. I was amused to see sugar sachets in the bedroom tea-making stuff marked Gulf Air and Air France (but why not?) but less amused to find the milk in Marvel powder sachets. I hate the stuff and surely those little tubs of UHT milk would be better. The bar in the basement is a little awkward, being a windowless room, but perhaps you could take your drink up to the more open reception area. We didn't try the restaurant for dinner, although it offered various Greek specialities at affordable prices that might have been interesting. Breakfast was a good and generous buffet, full English with those dishes beloved of Europeans also available (such as cold meat slices and various cakes and pastries) although the small plates hinted at a less generous attitude, as did the tomato sauce sachets which were somehow sticky and covered with the stuff outside. Had they been rescued from someone else's plate? Or maybe Gulf Air, if they came from the same place as the sugar sachets above, had suffered a decompression and tomato sauce sachets had whizzed round the cabin exploding? Imagine that – the passengers would have walked into the terminal as if covered in blood. I prefer to believe they had just got sticky by accident on this one occasion but have to report as I find. Anyway, the breakfast was good, and if you are shameless like me and go back for more until replete, totally adequate. *Sgl £65, dbl £95, inc b/fast.*

Sleeperz Hotel Station Rd; ☎ 01223 304050; e info@sleeperz.com; www.sleeprz.com
Budget job very convenient for station (but a good walk into town). Modern IKEAish look. *Sgl £39, dbl £59.*

BED & BREAKFAST Means what it says: a room in somebody's house. Usually you have to be out by a certain time in the morning and find your own dinner in the evening, but some are more flexible. Typically £29–60 per person per night. See tourist information.

APARTMENTS These may be purpose built, on the side of a hotel, or just somebody's flat. You have to cater for yourself but you usually have cooking facilities, washing machine, TV, shower etc without having to deal with hotel staff, so you have the freedom to come and go unencumbered and therefore privacy. Very competitive compared to full-on hotels, but obviously you don't get pampered. 'Serviced' means the place gets cleaned. See *Tourist information*, page 153.

SHOP ECCENTRIC

Central Cambridge is absolutely great for quirky little shops containing absolute gems, unbeatable for bookshops, and places you can find fashionable, individual outfits and accessories. True, there are the usual ghastly malls, such as Lion Yard and the Grafton Centre, and the usual chain stores, but useful though they may be, you won't find anything too eccentric there.

Here's a few suggestions:

FOR YOUNGSTERS Kids **Magic Joke Shop** (*29 Bridge St; \ 01223 353003; www.jokeshop.co.uk*) and the T-shirt shop opposite. Don't miss little All Saints' Passage which links Sidney and Trinity streets. Here is **The Chocolate House**. A notice in the window says: 'Warning: Unruly children will be kept and sold as slaves' (which could be a good result if you have any).

FOR FASHION-CONSCIOUS TEENS Try Market Street and Sidney Street for cheap jeans etc. Continue down to Bridge Street for **Fat Face** (*30B Bridge St; \ 01223 307630*) (on the right). The market itself for jeans, jewellery and hippie-goth stuff (obviously varies).

FOR DESIGN-CONSCIOUS ADULTS This is your perfect city. Try charming Green Street, Trinity Street, jewellery in All Saints' Passage and Rose Crescent, and

Catherine Jones next to the Round Church. Basically the whole triangle between Trinity Street, Sidney Street and Petty Cury/Market Place. Wander down all the side passages – because they're worth it, as someone's cosmetics ad nearly says.

FOR GOURMETS You know you're getting near the **Cambridge Cheese Company** in All Saints' Passage as the pong grabs you by the throat. Marvellous, unless you are an oriental who hates the pong of cheese (well some do, and may we return the compliment about some of their rotted tofu thingies deep fried on sidewalks) in which case stay very well clear. Actually a good general deli with excellent olives. **Chocolate House** nearby, and excellent delis all over the central area. Particularly recommended in the Italian deli field is **Limoncello**, away from the centre at 212 Mill Road (that's not just beyond the Narnian lamppost, and beyond the 'Tech' but also beyond the railway bridge – shudder!).

FOR BOOKSHOPS, NEW ... What a town for a bibliophile! The central area offers a massive **Borders** (*12–13 Market St;* ↘ *01223 306188*), a huge **Waterstones** (*22–24 Sidney St;* ↘ *01223 351688*) and the inimitable and rambling **Heffers** (*20 Trinity St;* ↘ *01223 568568*) plus branches in King Street (arts and graphic) and the Grafton Centre (children's and general). There is also a sizeable **WH Smith** (*14–15 Market St;* ↘ *01223 311313*) which is particularly good for stationery/magazines/news. And, of course, the official **Cambridge University Press** (*1 Trinity St;* ↘ *01223 333333*). The big bookstores all have their own cafés and toilets so you can settle in for the

day, really. Christian books at **Amana Books** in, appropriately, All Saints' Passage
(℡ *01223 366033*).

... AND BOOKSHOPS, OLD Still a very healthy second-hand book trade. Try the area
around **St Edward's Passage** (which runs between King's Parade and Peas Hill) and
also **Magdalene Street** (down Bridge Street). If the internet would seem to have
killed off many a small bookstore, then nothing replaces the joy of browsing in such
shops and holding the real books in your hands. It's like trying on shoes – wouldn't
you rather have the real thing in front of you, not a picture of it?

PHOTOGRAPHIC Green Street, King's Parade, Lion Yard.

TOURIST INFORMATION

The Cambridge Visitor Information Centre The Old Library, Wheeler St (behind Guildhall, which is the south
side of the Market); ℡ 01223 464732, for accommodation ℡ 01223 457581, for tours ℡ 01223 457574;
www.visitcambridge.org

7 Eccentric Walks

The essential Cambridge

A WALK ON THE MILD SIDE: THE BEST OF THE CITY

It's tiny. The vital stuff and absolute gems of Cambridge are contained within a thin isosceles triangle about 1,000 yards (1km) tall. The thin point is to the north, at Magdalene Bridge. The right (east) side runs straight from there down Bridge Street, Sidney Street and St Andrew's Street to the junction of the base of the triangle, Downing Street. The left (west) is the quintessential Cambridge street, running pretty well south from the fork with the other street at the top of the triangle into St John's Street, Trinity Street and King's Parade. The base is Pembroke Street and Downing Street, so the triangle is tilted slightly left (west) on the map.

All this means you can cover the essential Cambridge in a day on foot. Of course, you should include the Backs of the riverside colleges, which makes it a bit wider, and the baseline could be extended to Lensfield Road to include a couple more colleges and the Fitzwilliam Museum. But on the whole I'd stick to my guns and say that little triangle contained the vital ingredients and essential character and beauty of Cambridge. Not that you don't get surprised by more details after a lifetime knowing the place: there are always little quirks and turns you can discover, and there are plenty of bits beyond this triangle to keep an interested visitor busy for weeks. But the fact remains, missing this one bit would be like visiting New York without setting foot on Manhattan island.

I'm going to suggest a short walk taking in the best, and, although it's not a prescription, I have to say you will have failed to see Cambridge if you omit any of these things:

- A grand old college, by which you suddenly leave the hubbub and enter another world of ancient learning, with quiet courts (quadrangles) and gardens;
- The incomparable King's College Chapel;
- The quirky little shopping streets and alleyways connecting the two sides of the triangle near the top (north of the market);
- The river, its eccentric bridges and punting (doing or looking) and the Backs;
- The best pubs;
- The truly great architecture.

This walk will include all of these musts *except* the maze of little shopping streets – Rose Crescent, Green Street, All Saints' Passage etc. You are intelligent enough to buy this book, so you can find your own way round there. And King's Chapel, which on this walk is seen from the outside (hardly suggesting its glories inside) and is dealt with in another chapter (page 191). I suggest dealing with it on another occasion, or after a good lunch has rested you. It's too much to digest otherwise. There's only so much you can do in a comfortable morning or afternoon stroll.

JOINING THE WALK IF NOT ALREADY IN THE CITY (if so skip this whole section, unless you're a science history boff)

This starts at the **Eagle** pub in Bene't Street (see map). Of course you could join at any other point. Here are some directions for those coming from out of the city. If coming by rail, take the city bus which will be waiting, or will soon arrive, right outside the station entrance. It costs only £1. Get off in **Emmanuel Street** after the bus does a very sharp right turn (after about 2km). Walk back to the main road you've just turned off, turn right (loos in the Lion Yard shopping centre on the left if you need them), turn left into Petty Cury (a pedestrianised shopping street), go straight on (noting the pinnacles of King's Chapel peeping over the roofs ahead) past the Guildhall on your left with the market to your right (which you can peruse later), turn left into Peas Hill (nothing to do with peas nor a hill; see page 228) and turn right at Barclays bank at the end and there's the Eagle pub on the right.

If coming by coach (long-distance bus), you'll end up at Drummer Street, so just turn right into Emmanuel Street and proceed as above.

If coming by car, I strongly suggest parking at the Trumpington Park & Ride and catching the frequent very cheap buses from there. It's very close to the M11 junction with the A10 (for more about P&R, see page 236). By all means sit up top and enjoy the ride into the city but when it swings right into narrow Pembroke Street press the buzzer and come downstairs. The stop is further along in what has by then become Downing Street.

Walk back along the road the bus came on, on the same side as the stop, and take the small, unmarked lane about 300 yards (metres) along on your right. I say unmarked, but it is signed on the wall **Free School Lane** a few feet down, but unhelpfully not at the end. There *is* a sign saying Whipple Museum on the corner, however.

Note the science labs on your right on this lane. Unspectacular they may look, but spectacular have been the discoveries and achievements inside.

For one thing you may notice the plaque above a door to the memory of John Hopkinson and his son John Gustave Hopkinson. If you came to Cambridge by train, the electric motors were made possible by Hopkinson senior's work; if you came by sea, the ship was protected by lighthouse beams shone through lenses he designed. But if, eagle-eyed, you notice the plaque says they both died on the *same day* in 1898, father 49, son 18, you naturally wonder why. I can't fully give you the answer, nor can anyone. They were found dead with the two daughters of the family on a mountaineering holiday near a peak called Petite Dent de Veisivi in Switzerland. No-one has ever established precisely what happened.

As for father-and-son scientists, these **Cavendish laboratories** have had some great ones. William Henry Bragg, a Trinity scholar, won the Nobel Prize for Physics jointly with his son William Lawrence in 1915 (the only father and son to share such a prize). Yet another Cavendish laboratory father and son won the same prize three decades apart – Sir Joseph Thomson, discoverer of the electron (as mentioned on the wall further down) in 1906 and his son Sir George in 1937. Most of the research labs have now moved to more modern facilities elsewhere.

Further down there is a scrap of garden – this has a scientific connection too, for it is the only remaining part of the old **University Physic Garden** set up in 1761 to study the art of the old herbalists. In the 19th century this moved to the present Botanic Gardens site to make room for the laboratory studying the newer kind of physics.

At the end of Free School Lane, which turns into a pedestrian passage, complete with a sign banning cycling which is ignored on average 30 times an hour, you come out opposite the Eagle pub.

THE WALK AROUND CAMBRIDGE'S CROWN JEWELS Starting (and finishing) at the historic **Eagle** pub in Bene't Street, notice the high coaching inn entrance to the yard. You are also immediately faced with the pub's historic nature with the blue plaque about the discovery of DNA and the double helix structure of the code for life, announced by Crick and Watson right here in 1953. But it's a historic pub in many other ways, as we'll find at the end of this walk.

Facing the pub, turn to your left (west) and walk to the end of the street, pausing to examine the architecture of the oldest Cambridge church, St Bene't's. Notice the crudity of the arches in the tower, being Saxon.

Turn right into King's Parade to see the stately front of **King's College and Chapel** – known as a chapel with a small college attached for their disproportionate relationship – a classic view of Cambridge that must have greeted centuries and centuries of scholars, you might assume. You would be wrong.

In the early Middle Ages, there was a jumble of poor houses, lanes, slums and wharves which led down to the river from here, until it was cleared to make the King's College site. But even since then, there has been for most of the time another row of houses opposite the King's Parade shops on what is now the grassed front of the college. They were a typical medieval/Tudor jumble of half timbering, dormer windows, tall chimneys, mismatched gables and jettied floors (where the upstairs sticks quaintly out over the street, to make it easier to throw the contents of the chamber-pots not very quaintly into the gutters). Most of these were taken down in 1836, although some lingered until 1870. There was a Provost's Lodge opposite St Mary's Passage and in front of the College Chapel, and the old gate, near the northeast corner of the chapel, shows where the old entrance to the college was. The Lodge can't have been as scruffy back in 1564 as it became later, for Queen Elizabeth in that year took up residence there for a while on her visit to Cambridge. It was demolished in 1824.

Opposite St Edward's Passage, an inviting alley in the King's Parade frontage, was a large house owned by eccentric John Nicholson, known around town as 'Maps'. He ran a circulating library in the late 18th century and when knocking on customers' doors would cry 'Maps, Maps!' A Georgian GPS, as it were – very handy.

I really want to give you a full and enthusiastic description of **King's Chapel**, but it would get in the way of this walk, so it's on page 191. As I say there, the important thing is to contrast this with the crudity of St Bene't's church we just saw round the corner and – particularly when you get round to seeing the interior – marvel at how miraculously the stonemason's craft had moved on over the centuries. The plain exterior hardly hints, however, at the interior splendour.

Of course, feel free to divert into the chapel (which needs at least a whole hour of your attention), but assuming we stroll on, don't forget to go back another time. Missing it would be like going to Cairo and not seeing the pyramids, Agra and not seeing the Taj Mahal, to Penge and not seeing Penge East railway station... well, you get the idea.

The next building set back on the left is the **Senate House**, and on the right is the church of **Great St Mary's,** the university church. This is relatively plain compared to King's, although from the same era, but worth a look inside all the same. You can climb the tower for a small fee (£2) and I recommend that for anyone fit enough to use the stairs in a four-storey building. Don't go up the narrow spiral stairs with heavy bags, for you will want both hands free to cling to the stair rail on the way down. The lady on the reception desk may keep your bag while you make the ascent, and can see what you are doing in the tower top by CCTV, by the way, in case you are tempted to do a 'moonie' to the passing populace.

If you feel that this tower could kill you – and it probably won't but if you're over a certain age the 123 steps will leave you more breathless than Liz Hurley or Bruce

Willis ever did – then the notice in the bell chamber, if the door is open, will be off-putting. It says: 'Bells Up – Entering Invites Certain Death'. Say what you mean, don't sit on the fence chaps! Death is always certain, like taxation, I suppose.

If the bells ring while you're standing there, cover your ears, or don't bother going to the flute recital this afternoon. You won't hear much. Actually, as I recount in the churches section (page 203), this tower *did* kill one man – the chap who built it, hence the strange doggerel about the 'steeple's shame' just inside the doors at the base of the tower (marked private, ask permission from the desk to pop in for a second and it's high up on the wall behind you).

The reason for climbing the tower is to get a great orientating view of central Cambridge and to see how tiny the city is, or the bits that matter. You can look down on King's and many of the other colleges. But you can also see the green fields beyond Cambridge and how the M11 and the A45 run either side. You can look down on the market, and all the landmarks are helpfully identified on the tower top.

Continuing on, there's a rather good pair of **relief models of Cambridge**, labelled in Braille for the blind, so you can feel your way round the city. (Talking of relief, I notice the toilets in Cambridge have 'sharps disposal' chutes – council speak for junkies' syringes which may have Aids infection – marked in Braille, so the presumably vast population of blind HIV positive heroin users can dangerously fumble around with their infected needles. However, the nearby condom machines, which might prevent such infections, *don't* have Braille instructions. Funny old world.)

162

Meanwhile continue on up Trinity Street and have a look at the totally splendid gate of **Trinity College** on your left, and a glimpse of the Great Court within. If the statue of King Henry VIII has, as it did on my last visit, a table leg instead of a sceptre in his grasp, blame the students.

Go on down this lovely street (watching out for demon cyclists if you stand admiringly in the middle of the road), noting the inviting Rose Crescent, Green Street and All Saints' Passage on the right (worth a later visit for the shops), plus **Heffers** bookshop, one of the very best (with coffee bar and toilets).

Enter **St John's College** by another magnificent gateway on your left as you go along St John's Street (although by all means go further and merge with Bridge Street, take a look at Magdalene Bridge and come back).

The alternative, if St John's is closed, is to go through **Trinity** for marvellous courts and architecture (but a relatively boring chapel, to my taste), or **Clare** for fine gardens or **King's.** Or use Trinity Lane, the narrow road to the right beyond Trinity College, going back towards our start, turning right into Garret Hostel Lane to access the Backs without going through a college, or paying a fee, at all.

However, I strongly suggest St John's because it is beautiful, huge, interesting and relatively cheap to enter (£2.50). First, have a look at the extraordinary **gate tower** from across the road. The coat of arms is of foundress Lady Margaret Beaufort, who figures a lot in the Cambridge story. The beasts either side are, eccentrically, mythical yales, which have elephant's tails, antelope's bodies, goat's heads and useful swivelling horns. I say mythical, but my brother, after finishing the King Street Run (see page 144) once claimed to have seen one of these wandering around. There are at least two more yales in Cambridge, Christ's having a pair on its gate too, having the same foundress. Notice from the street the great size of the chapel roof (on the right looking towards the gate) of which more later.

There is a fan vault (ceiling), of which you can see a much better example at King's Chapel (and by the same mason, William Swayne), and the wooden gates display fine linen fold carving. You go in, pay the fee and are given a leaflet describing the superb five quadrangles, or rather courts, which make this college so impressive and their different architecture, so I'll leave that to them. The signed 'tourist route' (*so* crass, 'visitor route' would be more genteel – we're not mere *tourists*, we're learned travellers) takes you through the **Chapel**, which is well worth examining. Like the chapel at Exeter College, Oxford, it is insanely tall, is by the same architect, Sir George Gilbert Scott, a 19th-century Gothic revival nut, and is modelled on the same Paris church, Sainte-Chappelle. High Victorian fantasy, and well done.

However, there are other interesting older parts in the sort of ante chapel – not least the terrible toll of war dead that faces you as you come in. Notice the macabre double tomb of Hugh Ashton, showing him as a sculpture in rude health and full regalia lying in the top bunk, as it were, but in another sculpture below on the bottom bunk, an emaciated, wasted corpse. These *memento mori* devices were typical of the 16th and 17th centuries, reminding the living that they must prepare for the afterlife now.

Carved on the tomb and topping the railings around it is a rebus – a visual pun – on the name Ashton. A ton was a barrel, as in pubs called the Three Tuns, and here the joke is an ash tree growing through a barrel. I particularly noticed it because of seeing in St Bartholomew the Great in London's Smithfield (featured in *Four Weddings and a Funeral*) a rebus to a chap called Bolton, a crossbow bolt similarly splitting a barrel.

Leaving the rest of the courts for the leaflet to describe, you can't miss as you cross the river the beautiful **Bridge of Sighs** a few yards downstream (a copy of the wrong bridge in Venice, as is the same with the similarly misnamed one in Oxford over a street, but never mind).

From the bridge you are standing on you can usually see, looking straight down on the shadier side, how full of fish the Cam is. More amusingly, you can see looking upstream at the curve towards King's, how totally useless most tourists are at punting. If a punt has three or four Neanderthal types shouting as if they've been to the pub and/or three hopeless girlies screeching and giggling as they bash each other over the head with the pole, all standing up while the punt wobbles alarmingly, settle in for the show. It's funnier than the jumping dolphins at Sea World, but ends up the same – with the dumb animals back in the drink.

There, on the right as you cross the river, is yet another huge court of St John's, **New Court**, sitting there like a vast wedding cake plonked down for a posh nosh, or a huge Indian railway station or possibly a vast mental hospital. Ignore it, it's only 19th-century gothic pastiche and we can be snobby about that, having seen older courts and a far better gothic pastiche in the chapel. There are yet more fairly ghastly modern buildings beyond that and the interesting 800-year-old **School of Pythagoras** (see page 98).

Turn left instead along the riverside, past the inviting locked gate over a metal bridge (something to tell your psychoanalyst, surely) and follow the path round. Coming to a junction of paths, turn left towards the river and you are heading for the back of Trinity. Note the huge **Wren library** ahead of you, which reminds us that almost all English architecture in the last 2,000 years has been either Gothic or Classical, revived alternately. This is Classical at its best, built in 1695, and has the perfect proportions that Christopher Wren applied to St Paul's Cathedral and many London churches.

The pinkish stone was well chosen to catch the evening sun. It was also perfectly designed for function: the ground floor on the riverbank is designed to be floodable, elegantly holding up the upper floor where the library sits high and dry. The windows are large and sit higher than the bookcases set at right angles so natural light floods every part of the library all day. Even the furniture was designed by Wren, with ingenious rotating book stands in the reading tables, so you could compare four books at once.

166

You can visit the interior only if you have paid to visit Trinity College. You may indeed see a bowler-hatted porter, looking like one of those frightening chaps from *Clockwork Orange*, whose job it is to prevent your entering the back of the college without paying. Never fear, we are turning right, either right on the very riverside if you wish to reach the Trinity punting station and hire a boat, or alongside the lawn to reach the lane at the end. As you emerge on to Garret Hostel Lane and turn right, for goodness' sake watch out for cyclists who head off the humped bridge as if they were Lance Armstrong winning the Tour de France. But the bridge allows you to linger for a languorous look down on the aforesaid punting station and all the goings-on there. Looking back on your left you can see college gardens with students swotting in the sunshine (ideally).

After the bridge, turn left, parallel to the river again, (indeed on the path you would have been on had you not walked towards Trinity) and soon on the left is an entrance to **Clare College** (which has its own famous bridge – see page 72). However, don't do this right now but carry on to get the quintessential Cambridge view of the back of **King's** and its chapel, seen – it's always a surprise, this – over the heads of contented cattle munching grass in the riverside meadow, and with punters passing somewhere in between the bovine and the brilliant.

You can't enter King's from here, so carry on parallel to both the river and the road to your right, through some pleasant parkland and turn left when you reach a road (Silver Street), back towards the river. The college on your left is **Queens'** and as we cross the bridge by the **Anchor** pub (good downstairs bar with view of river and outside terrace) don't miss the **Mathematical Bridge** on your left (discussed on page 94) which joins the two halves of Queens'. There are three **punting stations** here, one on the upper part of the river beyond the point where it divides and there is a weir (down which fearless local children surf in hot weather, not advised).

The Anchor pub contains baby-changing facilities, but if yours is a red-faced furious one who won't be pacified, I'm afraid you can change only the nappy, not the baby.

You can also squeeze along the riverside to Mill Lane and more pubs, particularly the friendly **Mill** on the corner. The bit of grass across the bridge from the pub is Laundress Green, where the town's women used to hang their washing and chat.

Refreshed or not – there's always the Eagle, remember – head up to the top of Silver Street (or Mill Lane) and turn left and in a few yards you're back to Bene't Street on the right and the Eagle. I promised to tell you about it but I'm too tired and going in for a beer. The details are on page 143 instead.

SHOPPING AND CHANGING: A WALK FINDING TOWN, NOT GOWN

As stated above, the real charm of Cambridge the town is contained within the triangle of Sidney Street, Trinity Street and Downing/Pembroke Street. Just dive into the lanes and alleyways – particularly Green Street, All Saints' Passage and Rose Crescent near the north of this triangle, and also the lanes and alleyways between

King's Parade and the Guildhall – and you will find wonderful individual, even eccentric shops and places to eat of real charm instead of the usual national and international chain stores (which are nevertheless available aplenty in Lion Yard in Petty Cury on the southeast corner of the market, in Market Street off the northeast corner of the market or the Grafton Centre further afield). For a department store, you could try John Lewis (formerly Robert Sayle, I think) on St Andrews Street/Regent Street corner, which was being rebuilt as I write. More on shopping: page 151.

THE INESSENTIAL CAMBRIDGE: A STROLL UP KING STREET

King Street, which unnoticed takes off from the city centre at a furtive angle eastwards and immediately is flanked by unprepossessing buildings of indifferent architecture, is all the more rewarding when you give it a chance and find a real gem.

You find King Street off Sidney Street by taking the odd pedestrianised Sussex Street which links up with the narrow Hobson Street and seems to go nowhere. At this point, there's a wonderful music shop on the corner. You can buy bagpipes, and hire strange instruments with a mention of money back. Money back for what – playing badly?

Looking left from the end of Sussex Street, the road does a right-angled jink to the right and at this point offers some less than lovely buildings. Stick with it and it's worth it in an understated way.

There's a less than posh (at the time of writing) boozer called **The Cambridge Arms** (though 'all meals under £3' must be welcome to hungry students). On the other side is **The Bun Shop**, another well-known student bar/tapas joint, despite its misleading name. Press on and the road becomes charming, in that kind of not-too-grand, almost-but-not-quite-poor, low-rise way that East Anglia does. You pass a good tea and coffee shop (the ground stuff in bags, not another Costa Wotsitbucks) and **Clown's Café** is also great for a sit down. The **Champion Of The Thames** pub is just charming and thoroughly recommended (and off the tourist trail), the long-winded notice on the far end almost absurd.

There's a more garish pub called **The King Street Run** (which is also the name of a strange boozing race down this street) which wouldn't look out of place in Blackpool or Brighton, and no end of elegant little houses, with a few alleyways through to Christ's Pieces (a park, not a holy relic) on the right. Heaps of barbers (Cambridge has more coffee shops and barber's shops than is reasonable, a bald teetotaller told me).

Some almshouses further down were the gift of a Joseph Merill (they always tell you about their generosity at great length, and thereby buy immortality, but why not?). Some complicated formula of giving £1,667 at 3% explained on the plaque is beyond my poor maths, after trying the aforementioned pubs, but the bevelled brickwork about the windows in very fine. The bevel is in the detail.

Further up is a discreet art gallery, **Broughton House**, another passage called Pike's Walk, and soon on the left more almshouses. These were created by the generous will of Elizabeth Knight in 1647 who gave these six houses (well, not these, for they are 1880 replacements) and '18 pounds per annum to be equally divided amongst those that shall inhabit them'.

At the end on the left is the most extraordinary pub in the street, the **St Radegund**, shoehorned into an odd scrap of ground. Its odd story involves a saint and a well. Should you need a loo, don't despair, there's one on Midsummer Common if you walk out of the end of the road and cross the main road. If you want to get back to the city centre, Jesus Lane on the left goes that way but is frankly rather dull. Best go back the way you came. The very odd geography of these narrow roads is clearly down to the huge colleges they thread between.

8 Eccentric Things to See or Do

Eccentric exhibits and other entertainments

CAMBRIDGE'S ECCENTRIC MUSEUMS

Listed somewhat facetiously by their oddest or silliest things (see proper name in bold, curators PLEASE keep a sense of humour ...). Actually, perhaps the Cambridge Curatorial Comedy Club, or CCCC, meets somewhere secret on Mondays, for the museums are mostly (but not all) closed on that day.

MUSEUM OF QING GOES DING! Try not to make your entrance to this august institution, **The Fitzwilliam Museum** (*Trumpington St;* ❧ *01223 33900; www.fitzwilliammuseum.cam.ac.uk. Open Tue–Sat 10.00–17.00; Sun and bank hol Mon noon–17.00; closed non-hol Mon. Admission free*) as one bumbling visitor did early in 2006. He tumbled down the stairs and hit three almost priceless Qing dynasty vases. He ended up sprawling across the floor surrounded by countless shards of ancient ceramics. It was a curator's nightmare.

Another visitor was quoted as saying: 'We watched the man fall as if in slow motion. He landed in the middle of the vases and they splintered into a thousand pieces.' There was a moment's terrible silence while it sank in. Then the man, still lying on the floor, pointed to his shoelace and said: 'There it is, that's the culprit.'

The vases were estimated as worth £75,000, and the visitor – a villager from Fowlmere – was banned from the museum.

Be that as it may, I find when I smash my own not very good pottery that it's interesting to see how thin you managed to make mugs and bowls. You want them to be as light as possible without collapsing on the wheel. I bet the Qing ones were a lot thinner. Not much consolation, of course, to the Fitzwilliam staff, who were determined to glue the vases back together with immense patience.

A total philistine would ask what use most vases are anyway. In fact, I have a few totally ghastly ones I can never quite bring myself to smash given to me by relatives. If that villager wants to pop round sometime …

Having had some fun with a silly story, I must point out that this is one of the world's great galleries of fine art with a superb collection that can't be detailed here. Marvellous collection of manuscripts going back to illuminated texts from the Middle Ages (wonderful stuff including the Macclesfield Psalter depicting scenes from 1320s England – although note that this psalter is not often on display). Allow at least a couple of hours per visit, and it's worth several. Well set up for children's exploration (as long as they do up their shoelaces) and a great website.

MUSEUM OF DRAINAGE (PRICKWILLOW) It sounds like a museum of U-bends and pipes, but is not that eccentric, being the **Museum of Fenland Drainage** (*Main St, Prickwillow, near Ely; go east from Ely through Queen Adelaide (yes, that is a place) on the B1382;* ✆ *01353 688360; www.prickwillow-engine-museum.co.uk. Open Apr & Oct*

Sat–Sun 13.00–16.00; May–Sep Fri–Tue 13.00–16.30; closed Nov–Mar; running days – about six a year – best for visit: contact museum or see website. Admission £3 per adult, a little more on running days) and drainage engines, in particular. OK, you might think this is of limited interest, but if you love old machinery, it's fascinating. You should see the flames leap up when they start up some of these old engines. Naturally it's important in this part of the world where the marshy fens once meant that many places such as Ely were islands. Drainage of these marshes – which once provided hideouts for rebels and bandits – produced the fertile flatlands of East Anglia, although one bizarre side effect is that the ground shrunk vertically, and therefore in some places the river is well *above* the surrounding land. The rivers need to maintain their original height, of course, or else they would flow from the sea not the other way round (one in Norfolk, the Thurne, has reversed its direction completely but reaches the sea by another route). So water had to be pumped up into the rivers.

Further north this was often done by the windmills all along the rivers (which were, in fact, windpumps) but further south the huge drainage pumps were part of the landscape. At first they were coal fired and steam driven (one of these is preserved at Stretham, see below), then oil- and petrol-driven ones took over (and these are mainly the ones this museum has rescued from around the fens) before electricity made it even easier. And if you like old British engineering, here you can see these engines, and running too (check days for running). The engines are housed in an old pump house on the banks of the River Lark. Plus there is much information about the related fenland history.

MUSEUM OF A STEAM-POWERED DOUBLE-ACTING ROTATIVE BEAM ENGINE Catch another drain. Some 15 minutes out from Cambridge city centre, in the flat landscape of the Fens, is **Stretham Old Engine** (*Stretham, near Ely;* ☏ *01353 648578. Open second Sun of the month and bank hol Mon from Good Friday to Aug bank hol 11.30–17.00. Admission £2 adults, £1 children/OAPs)* one of the old steam pumping engines which drained the marshes of old to make the farmland of today, before they were replaced by diesel, then electric pumps.

You'll see the tall chimney before you reach the place. Once inside, look at the Victorian machinery (the engine was built over 150 years ago), and then visit Stoker's Cottage next door with its display on the history of fen drainage. The huge engine is worked by an electric motor nowadays, which is a bit like the tail wagging the dog (or the bog in this case), but never mind. You can learn interesting stuff like how in 1892 the crankshaft was replaced …

MUSEUM OF COMPLETE DARKNESS This is one of those odd little museums all over Britain that make such fascinating visiting (and a bit shorter than the Victoria & Albert). The **Blacked-Out Britain War Museum** (*1 St Mary's St, Huntingdon;* ☏ *01480 450998. Open Mon–Sat 09.00–17.00, Sun 10.00–14.00. Admission free)* is a personal collection relating to the Home Front 1939–45 but is open to the public at Huntingdon Trading Post (antiques centre). Everything from dried eggs to mortar bombs if you wanted to see how a previous generation managed not that long ago. If you hear a siren, just dive under the stairs …

8

THE MUSEUM THAT NEEDS OLD BATS Not a museum at all. The **Cambridge University Botanic Garden** (*Bateman St;* ✆ *01223 336265; and www.botanic.cam.ac.uk. Open Apr–Sep 10.00–18.00; Feb, Mar, Oct 10.00–17.00; Nov–Jan 10.00–16.00. Admission £3*) has in early spring an extraordinary plant in bloom called the jade vine. Jade, I suppose, not because it looks like some character off the telly but because of its lurid and enormous jade-coloured flower spikes, the particular hue of blue/green devised by nature to attract passing bats at dusk in their native Philippines forest to pollinate them. How many large old bats are passing in Cambridge is open to question. No it's not, there are plenty, but are they *suitable*?

Here are glasshouses, an arboretum, grass maze, rare species of plants from around the world etc, café, all in 40 acres of landscaped gardens and it's just a pleasant place to wander round at most times of the year, plus there are learned talks and walks at various times.

The Botanic Garden is between Trumpington Road (that leads out of the city to the south from King's Parade) and Hills Road (at the point where Station Road branches off). The east–west road linking these two thoroughfares at the north end of the gardens is Bateman Street, and there is an entrance on this street and on Hills Road near Station Road.

MUSEUM OF FAILURE Well, that's a bit harsh, it's actually the **Scott Polar Research Institute** (*Lensfield Rd, Cambridge;* ✆ *01223 336540; www.spri.cam.ac.uk. Open Tue–Sat 14.30–16.00. Admission free*) named after British explorer Robert Falcon

Scott, who died in Antarctica in 1912 after reaching the South Pole. It was set up eight years later as a tribute. Yes, he reached the South Pole but famously didn't make it back again. We were all taught at school what heroes these chaps were, and how Oates said to Scott before sacrificing himself to try to save the others: 'I'm just going outside, I may be some time.'

Scott wrote in his increasingly shaky writing: 'Had we lived, I should have had a tale of hardihood, endurance, and courage of my companions which would have stirred the heart of every Englishman.' And, of course, that did stir hearts. When you get to the final 'For God's sake, look after our people' you would be cold indeed not to shed the odd tear.

On closer examination Scott appears to have been a complete prat. He ignored all good advice. Oates was injured and didn't want to go, the cult of the British amateur meant they didn't ski and used 'manly' man-hauling while the Norwegian Amundsen, who had studied people who live in such conditions, skied to beat Scott there (and back). Scott also diverted their expedition to go and look at some rocks for a day or two and even got the chaps to haul the rock samples back with them.

Shackleton, on the other hand, got all his men back safely after his ship was crushed by ice a few years later, but his superb feat of sailing across the southern oceans in a small boat to get rescuers was ignored because World War I had started and Britain needed romantic *dead* heroes, not live ones. That's the revisionist view.

The revision of the revision is the recent one that the weather that caught Scott and his team out was a once-in-a-hundred-years storm and but for that they would have made it back, as they so nearly did. But for all that, one must add, they still would have been beaten by the Norwegians. We Brits love heroic failure for some reason – why do we remember *Titanic* and forget her two sister ships? Why do we like Tim Henman at Wimbledon (I hope that comment is outdated by the time you read this, but I doubt it)? Meanwhile, a book called *Captain Scott* by Ranulph Fiennes, who knows a thing or two about exploring the Antarctic, argues that Scott has been traduced in recent years and was in fact the hero we thought he was in the first place. Go and have a look and make up your own mind. If it's snowing hard, for goodness sake set off home before the Norwegians do.

MUSEUM OF SOME GEEZER'S HOUSE This is the superbly eccentric **Kettle's Yard** on Castle Street (☏ *01223 352124; www.kettlesyard.co.uk. Open 1 Apr–1 Oct Tue–Sun and bank hol Mon 13.33–16.30; winter Tue–Sun and bank hol Mon 14.00–16.00)* Much recommended. A chap called Jim Ede, who was a curator of the Tate Gallery, London, once lived here with his wife Helen. Evidently he took his work home at weekends. The pair of them collected marvellous works by artists of their era, the early 20th century, and stuffed their house with well-chosen paintings, sculpture and knick-knacks. They left the lot to Cambridge. What is pleasantly eccentric is that you approach what seems to be a small cottage, ring the bell and are admitted with barely a word. Nobody shows you round – you just wander through what turns out to be quite a large house. No labels, themes or explanations, no audio visual guide, no tea rooms or Kettle's Yard snowdomes or Kettle's Yard pencil sharpeners.

Marvellous – and you have the feeling of the personality of the couple, as if they've gone off to Southwold for a beach holiday and you're borrowing the place: the way they arranged pebbles in a spiral, that kind of thing. There are certainly artists you have heard of, such as Henry Moore and Barbara Hepworth, but it is the ones you don't expect that will be an education – don't miss the attic, for example.

MUSEUM OF BROKEN CLOCKS The Rupert Brooke Museum is at The Orchard, 45–47 Mill Way, Grantchester *(↘ 01223 845788; www.rupertbrooke.com. Admission free – but you should try the teas)* The broken clocks angle refers to the lines of his poetry:

> Stands the Church clock at ten to three?
> And is there honey still for tea?

The answer may well be yes to the latter, possibly both. Brooke is thoroughly discussed on page 33. This little museum is in the grounds of Orchard House near the Tea Garden and Pavilion, and contains words and photographs and some objects from Brooke's short life.

MUSEUM OF TALLY HO, GINGER! East Anglia was absolutely stuffed with air bases in World War II, both British and American – it was the 'unsinkable aircraft carrier', as Hitler found out to his cost – and you get some of that flavour at the back bar at the Eagle pub in Cambridge (page 143), or more sadly, at the American cemetery at

Madingley. Examples of the planes that survived the war ended up at the Imperial War Museum, Duxford, and someone of absolute brilliance had the brainwave not to hang them from ceilings of dusty galleries like so many giant Airfix kits, but actually to fly the things, just as the National Railway Museum at York does with steam engines (well, not flying them in that case, that would require a very long run-up and a cliff).

Here at **The Imperial War Museum** (✆ *01223 835000; duxford.iwm.org.uk. Open daily Nov–Mar 10.00–16.00, Apr–Oct 10.00–18.00; last admission 45 min before closure; closed 24–26 Dec. Admission adult £13, children free, various concessions)* at Duxford, close to Cambridge, you can see every kind of plane from World War I biplanes to Concorde and the finest collection of American aircraft outside the United States, plus naval aircraft from past conflicts. It is really too much to do justice to here and even if you're not a fully paid-up *aeronak*, is a worthwhile day out. Particularly on the flying days and air shows. Cue old gits making corny jokes to their embarrassed offspring like speaking into their imaginary facemasks: 'Bandits, four o'clock, wingco!' 'That's spiffing, Algy, it's only lunchtime now!'

Unfortunately, flying these old crates is not without risk – some of the planes frankly weren't very good when new – and there have been accidents. In 2002–03 there was spate of prangs, with a Bristol Blenheim bomber bellyflopping next to the M11, a Fairey Firefly crashing in a wheatfield (killing two men), an ex-Soviet jet trainer sliding on to the M11 through the fence, and an Albatross coming down in fields near the museum. Previously, a Harvard crashed in 2001, the last working Me109 crashed in 1997, and a P38 Lightning crashed in 1996, killing the pilot.

You don't need the Luftwaffe to make this stuff dangerous, it seems. The crews who take these vintage planes up know the dangers but love doing it nevertheless. Every precaution is made to avoid danger to the public.

The museum is reached by car at the M11 Junction 10 where it crosses the A505 Luton–Baldock–Newmarket road. By bus C7 from Emmanuel Street, Cambridge railway station and Addenbrooke's Hospital. Nearest station Whittlesford on the London Liverpool Street–Cambridge line but that would mean more than a mile to walk.

MUSEUM OF CREAKY FLOORS AND HOT WATER BOTTLES Excellent for rainy summer Mondays (when most other museums are shut), the **Cambridge and County Folk Museum** (*2–3 Castle St;* ☎ *01223 355159; www.folkmuseum.org.uk. Open Mon–Sat 10.30–17.00, Sun 14.00–17.00; closed Mon Oct–Mar. Adult admission £3*) is about the ordinary stuff of ordinary people's lives, and is therefore fascinating, and entertaining for those who can remember such ancient brands and appliances as well as for the young, who find them hilarious. The building itself is pleasantly ramshackle, being the former White Horse Inn (dating from 1600). Part of one wall is uncovered so you can see how the wattle and daub walls were made – the technology of mud huts, really. There are various bonkers household devices such as pressure cookers built like nuclear flasks, mousetraps of such devious cruelty they would squash or decapitate several at once, and everything about how our ancestors played, worked, cooked, drank, created art and dealt with pests.

MUSEUM OF CALCULATORS A concept that might not seem to add up (groan) but actually the **Whipple Museum of the History of Science** (*Free School Lane;* ☏ *01223 334500. Open Mon–Fri 12.30–16.30. Admission free*) is rather fascinating. If you're much below 50 you probably never used the weird slide rules and log tables schoolchildren were tortured with (log chairs would be worse) until electronic calculators came along, and, of course, mechanical calculators make another whole division. What you have here is a world-class collection of scientific instruments and models, and their roots. Actually, these places seem to multiply as there's a similar one at Oxford. To subtract a little, if Henry Latham (page 134) ever mentioned 'Whipple' he was probably talking about ice cream, whaspberry whipple.

PUNTING: PAIN OR PLEASURE?

A PRETTY POINTLESS DIGRESSION BEFORE PUNTING You don't need a travel guide to work out that the River Cam has a bridge at Cambridge, or indeed that an Ox can ford at Oxford. The links are more complex than that both cities are defined by a river crossing, however. Both rivers are called by Latin-derived names by pedants (and these universities could be called Pedants 'R' Us): the Cam is correctly, say some, the *Granta* above Silver Street Bridge and the Thames becomes the *Isis* miraculously only within the city of Oxford.

But, although both universities offer the pleasures of punting and rowing, they have very different rivers, the Thames being wider and deeper, allowing side-by-side rowing races. Cambridge, with its narrower, twisting river, has therefore evolved the curious races known as the Bumps, where a boat bumps the one ahead in a fore and aft race. There are two sets of such races: Lenten ones (before Easter, that is), and the May Week ones, famously a fortnight in June (but they were once a week in May, honest!).

Students sometimes mount expeditions in search of the source of the Cam, and at least once this has included men in boats with pith helmets and witchdoctors, etc. Actually, it would be funnier if they were Africans, regarding the natives with deep suspicion and perhaps meeting another African chap coming the other way near Baldock for a 'Dr Livingstone, I presume' moment. Anyway, these expeditions invariably don't reach the source but end up at Grantchester where food and drink beckon, a good destination for an up-river punt. (This bit can also be defined as the Upper River, and there's the Middle River in the town and the Lower River beyond.)

If the students had pursued the Cam to its source, they might have (there are several branches) ended up at a charming spring beside the main street in the equally charming village of **Ashwell**, Hertfordshire (just over the Cambridgeshire border) which is found on the railway line from Cambridge to King's Cross or the A505 road from Royston to Baldock.

When I say 'on', I mean a few miles north of both, and the railway builders' optimism in calling the station 'Ashwell and Morden' was presumptuous to put it mildly, as I found plodding up the long lane to cover a meeting of Ashwell Parish Council as a cub reporter many, many decades ago. Among the useless facts I heard at their interminable, suicidally boring meetings was that the spring which is the, or a, source of the Cam contains some Ice Age beasties which seem not to have noticed that the glaciers have gone. Watch out for possible woolly mammoths and sabre-toothed tigers if you visit this recommended rather charming and sleepy hideaway (good pubs).

The Cam doesn't even reach the sea. It merges with the Great Ouse (pronounced to rhyme with booze, not louse) near Ely and eventually comes out in the Wash (as your granny may have said most things do). It thus carefully avoids mixing with Oxford's water, the watershed with the top edge of the Thames basin being just south of the above-mentioned Ashwell.

PUNTING: PLEASURE OR HUMILIATION? Punting if done well is a supremely elegant and efficient way of getting along the Cam, or Granta if you insist. It is Cambridge's answer to the gondoliers of Venice. In the idealised image, a lady in a pretty summer dress reclines on the cushions holding a parasol, for the sun beams down and flowers nod over the water. A man in blazer and straw boater stands on the flat end making the punt glide along with minimum fuss (the curved end, if there is one, is for Oxford cissies, after all). A wind-up gramophone warbles in the middle, next to an ice bucket with a bottle of champers. A wicker hamper contains elegant sandwiches with the crusts cut off.

The reality is often somewhat different. The geeky tourist goon drives his pole into the mud and pushes. The boat moves away from under him. The goon clutches panic-stricken to the pole now locked in the mud and is left stretching out over the increasing span of water until he is doing a bad impersonation of the Golden Gate

Bridge. The boat either shoots away or the pole begins to come out and the inevitable splash is greeted by wild cheers from onlookers. The water feels freezing at most times of the year, and the mud is vile.

As 'any fule kno' you can't propel something from behind and above without making it deviate all over the show, and that's what your average tourist does. Or as physics undergrads might put it, 'the built-in self-magnifying fundamental error inherent instability factor' which means you might end up on your fundament and all errors will be self-magnified until disaster ensues.

Added to their embarrassment is the warning to pick the Cambridge end (squared off not rounded, Oxford ends) to punt from, whereas most punts are now double Cambridge ended. Confused? Fear not! Read on…

THE AVERAGE PUNTER'S GUIDE TO AVOIDING TOTAL HUMILIATION

- Do not overcrowd the punt.
- Do not get drunk before or during the trip.
- Do not take non-swimmers without buoyancy aids, huge dogs, horses or any kind of cattle. No I *don't* mean take non-swimmers *with* horses or cattle. Oh, never mind. Just don't.
- Do not stand up in the boat unless punting.
- Check that the pole is smooth and splinter-free before you leave. It needs to slide through your hands hundreds of times, so change it if it isn't. Make sure you also have a paddle, or something to paddle with (see below).

Now, standing on the square-ended platform with the rest of the punt before you, facing the direction you wish to go in, raise the pole until it is pointing up in the air at perhaps an 80° angle, that is tilting slightly from the vertical at the top in the direction of travel. Allow the pole to drop through your hands right beside where you are standing, almost scraping the punt, until it hits the bottom of the river. Push so the punt goes forward and your hands climb up the pole. As you reach the end of the pole free it with a slight twisting movement (to avoid getting stuck in mud) and repeat. Given the above-mentioned built-in self-magnifying fundamental error inherent instability factor, the whole thing will now go horribly wrong unless you apply the following clever bit. *Steering* is achieved by using the pole as a rudder while passing it up through your hands again to the starting position. It should stay on the same side of the punt, however. Swish its end in the water behind you to the side you wish the front of the punt to turn. It is extremely satisfying if well done. And extremely funny if not.

PUNTING: INFREQUENTLY ASKED QUESTIONS
Is it possible to punt from Cambridge to Oxford or vice versa?
Yes. It is possible, and being eccentric and being in England, it is probable. A team of scientists from Christ Church, Oxford, made the trip in 1971. Two punts made the 200-mile journey to Cambridge (it's only 85 miles by road) to raise money for charity.

They went from Magdalen Bridge to Magdalene Bridge via the Grand Union Canal, the River Ouse, through Bedford, Godmanchester, St Ives and on to the River

Cam, arriving in Cambridge after 13 days and many blisters. The effort was repeated in 2004 by Steven Holmes and a team from New College, Oxford, who counted 204 miles, through 115 locks in 12 days. If this carries on, there will be more punts in Cambridge than Oxford, so kindly punt some the other way.

What if you can't find the bottom?

You have gone too far, and are in the North Sea. Don't panic. Switch on navigation lights and practise your Danish.

What if the pole gets stuck?

If you're a complete twerp or having a laugh, hang on. Otherwise, let go and paddle back. They never stay stuck.

What if I can't raise the pole?

You may be under a bridge.

What if my pole disappears or won't move?

You are under Clare Bridge (the one with balls on), and students sometimes grab them for a lark.

Where's the best place to go?

Along the river, it's harder on the road.

No, seriously.
The best sights are in the Middle River, that is between Silver Street and Magdalene Bridge. But this is also the most crowded, so if you want a peaceful day out with picnic etc, try the upper river and head for Grantchester. There's just one spot that's too deep for punting and, tee-hee, it's got nettles on the bank which you discover after your pole fails to hit the bottom. Stay on the inside of the bend and you'll survive. The Lower River, below Jesus lock, is best known for rowing.

What about making love in a punt?
Making love in a punt needs cushions and privacy, both usually in short supply. Keep clear of weirs etc and be careful where you put your pole (it can drift away). Actually, 'making love in a punt' was a nickname for an unpopular beer when I was a student. No, I'm not going to spell it out for you.

Or making war?
Rumour has it that during the last war there was an armoured punt on Home Guard duty. It seems *Dad's Army* ludicrous – 'It's sinking, Captain Mainwaring.' 'Stupid boy, Pike' – and about as dangerous to the expected German *blitzkrieg* as the Romney, Hythe and Dymchurch Railway's miniature armoured train of the same era, which could have been derailed with a standard German army sausage.

On the other hand, punts have for centuries been armed in the fens near here. Massive punt guns were installed and the things looking like miniature one-gunned warships crept towards flocks of birds in boggy marshes, a cartridge more like an artillery shell in its breech, the gunner prostrate to avoid alarming the birds. A huge boom rent the air amidst much squawking, leaving a cloud of smoke, hundreds of dead and dying fowl, and the punt and its stunned, blackened and deafened occupant zipping backwards, if not sinking. Not very gentlemanly. Don't try it under Magdalene Bridge.

That sounds fun. Are torpedoes allowed in inter-punt warfare?

They aren't specifically banned but all Royal Navy torpedoes run too deep to hit a punt. If you want to mess around in this way – and I'm not *at all* recommending it – then high-powered water pistols and water bombs (small balloons from toy shops) are a possibility. You will need to fill those from a tap and carry them in a carrier bag, not that I've ever been so childish, of course, whereas the water pistols can be refilled as you go along.

PUNTING LOCATIONS There are three punt stations at the bottom of Mill Lane and Silver Street, one giving access to the upper river to Grantchester, the other two suitable for seeing the Backs and the famous bridges. There is also Trinity Punt

Station, down Trinity Lane to Garret Hostel Lane. Another is at Quayside, beside Magdalene Bridge, from which you can attack the Backs from the other direction (and be sure of drifting back to your starting point eventually however bad you are).

ECCENTRIC GOINGS-ON AROUND CAMBRIDGE

January	Straw Bear Festival, Whittlesey
February	Rag Week
March	Oxford v Cambridge Boat Race
Easter	Race of the Bogmen and Egg Throwing, Great Finborough, Suffolk.
May	Reach Fair Penny Throwing; Stilton Cheese Rolling, Stilton
June	Strawberry Fair, Midsummer Common
July	World Pea Shooting Championships, Witcham, Ely; World Snail Racing Championships, Congham, Norfolk
September	Dragon Boat Festival, Fen Ditton; Pumpkin Fayre, Soham
October	World Conker Championships, Ashton near Peterborough
December	Nine Lessons and Carols, King's Chapel

More details in companion book *Eccentric Britain*.

9 Eccentric Churches

Worship eccentrically

KING'S CHAPEL: A MIRACLE OF MASONRY

A RATHER IMPORTANT 'SHED' If you know of only one building in Cambridge before visiting, it will probably be this one. If you visit only one building in Cambridge, it should be this one.

Like the Taj Mahal, it is known by millions of postcards and posters of the perfect view from the Backs (the river side). Equally visible from King's Parade, the chapel is also known for its fabulous interior because of the Festival of Nine Lessons and Carols, broadcast to many parts of the world each Christmas Eve.

It is a sensational, brilliant building, in some ways the climax of 1,500 years of progression from Roman to Saxon to Norman to Gothic – from the Dark Ages to the Middle Ages – in increasing skill, the finest hour of such stonemasonry before the Renaissance's Classical revival turned to domes and pillars and pediment …

And yet … it is only a chapel, not a major cathedral.

Cambridge doesn't have a cathedral, as Ely serves for this purpose. So this chapel doesn't have huge transepts like York Minster, or spires like Salisbury, or towers like Westminster Abbey, or side aisles like Winchester. It is, in fact, modelled on the choir part of a cathedral, so you are looking at just one section, as it were, of a full-sized religious building, because just a chapel was needed. Nevertheless, for a college originally intended to have 70 scholars, it was an unnecessarily huge chapel, and King's has been described as 'a good chapel with a small college attached'.

It is, when all is said and done, a simple shed. Yes, everything outside leads upwards in parallel lines, as this is the Perpendicular phase of English Gothic, but it has a boxy rectangular plan, as mere chapels are meant to have. If it opened at one end it would do fine for storing a medium sized zeppelin. A shed, in shape maybe ... but look at the glory inside: hey, some shed!

To appreciate the technical perfection in the miracle of masonry that is King's Chapel, turn your back on it (assuming you are standing on King's Parade, with the row of shops behind you). Pop down to the right-hand (south) end of the row of shops, and left just a few yards up Bene't Street.

Here on the right is **St Bene't's church** (it is an abbreviation of St Benedict's; we Benedicts notice these things) and you don't need to go inside (although why not?) to appreciate the point of this small diversion. This is one of the oldest churches in Cambridgeshire, indeed some say *the* oldest. The tower is Saxon, that is pre-1066.

Look at the windows halfway up the tower. These are typical of the era. Roughly hewn, in a clumsy thick rubble wall. Windows of that era often had short, round arches through which a man could just squeeze. No glass, usually, so small was good to keep the rain and draughts out. Small also, however, because they technically couldn't make bigger ones. They had inherited the round arch of the Romans, but they couldn't build as well as they had, or dress the stones so finely. Civilisation had gone backwards. Dark Ages, indeed, for dimly lit interiors were filled with smoke and soot from rush lights and tallow candles (if you could afford them).

On the ground floor of this church, in what is probably a post-Saxon extension, we see later windows. The finer stone mullions (window dividers, except in Glasgow, where it's a very large number) and arrival of the pointed Gothic arch meant windows could be built higher and wider, letting more light into the interior, and allowing some scope for stained-glass windows. Many an English church has later style windows added, in an attempt to keep up with fashion, perhaps, but still for most of the Middle Ages the walls were thick and much more stone than glass.

Building higher, nearer to God and grander, was possible as the architects grew in skill and confidence, but not a few European churches collapsed because of the problem of transferring the sideways thrust of the roof down into the ground.

Turning back to King's Chapel, you can see you needed heavy buttresses to achieve this. Pinnacles on each buttress look like ornaments: in fact, they help divert the forces downwards (and are so prominent that the chapel has been likened to a giant sow on her back). In some churches flying buttresses (even double, or at Seville treble ones) achieved this task of taking the weight of the roof, yet here at Cambridge the impossible has been achieved – a high roof, of considerable weight because it also has stone vaulting beneath it, but no flying buttresses.

Yet from the interior we have progressed from that gloomy Saxon squatness, with tiny, crude windows, to a soaring majesty of height with walls mostly of glass. Amazingly, this apparently lightweight skin holds up not only the roof itself, which is the usual Toblerone shape, but also the fan vaulting. Vaulting (the interior ceiling) too had been increasing in complexity and skill. The Normans knew just the round half barrel vault the Romans had used, hence Romanesque. By intersecting two of these vaults, medieval architects found they could make a more interesting shape. The use of stone ribs allowed this to become increasingly complex yet light, and as with the windows the pointed arch allowed more and more height.

The end of this evolution is here above your head: the most extreme version of the relatively lightweight **fan vaulting**. This breathtaking display is the finest example in the world. See how cleverly those thin ribs take the forces of the roof down a conoid shape to the massive buttresses hidden beyond the walls. The rest of the walls don't hold up anything except themselves and their massive windows – they could just as well be open to the air like a Dutch barn. I say 'relatively lightweight' because the vaulting alone is thought to weigh well over 1,500 tons – a wooden ceiling would have been far lighter. Don't think about all that stone too much as you sit beneath gazing up at it.

Or, if you like the shiver which that remark gives you, consider that the stones merely rest on each other, having no strength at all until the arches were complete, being totally collapsible until the last stone was in place. This may have been behind Sir Christopher Wren's remark about this chapel in the century after its completion. Wren, of course, was the master of all things Classical revival, with the Sheldonian Theatre at Oxford, St Paul's in London and here in Cambridge the Trinity College library, and hardly a Gothic arch or vault among them.

He was said to have visited King's Chapel (then, of course, out of fashion) to marvel at the fan vaulting, and, contemporaries recorded, remarked to those who preferred the older style: 'If any man would show me where to place the first stone, I will build such another.'

That's exactly it. If they will all fall down until the last one is in place, where in heaven's name do you start?

A SHORT HISTORY AND ANOTHER MIRACLE King of self-importance Henry VIII typically gets his statue on the frontage – nearly opposite Bene't Street – but it was an earlier king of that name, **Henry VI**, who founded King's in 1441 and intended it exclusively for scholars from his other creation, Eton College near Windsor. (King's now admits students from anywhere, by the way.)

At both sites he wanted the chapel to be the first thing finished. At Cambridge there was a warren of riverside wharves and lanes in a typical unplanned medieval jumble of houses which he had swept out of the way to create the site for King's.

Henry became embroiled in the Wars of the Roses, and the chapel's history reflects this turbulent power struggle. The change in the limestone halfway up the walls shows where work stopped in 1461 when Henry was defeated and taken prisoner (the later stone coming from a different quarry).

Henry VI was murdered in the Tower of London in 1471. He became one saint, lost two kingdoms (England and France), founded two great colleges, and ended up in three parts (according to Shakespeare's *Henry VI Part One* etc (see Queens', page 93).

By the way, Henry VI wanted the chapel fairly plain and free from ornament, which is hardly how things turned out.

The next king, Edward IV, did little to finish the King's Chapel, but Richard III pushed the building ahead, with several bays of the chapel finished by the time the supposedly villainous evil old hunchback was killed in the 'my kingdom for a horse' scene at the Battle of Bosworth in 1485. I say 'supposedly' because the legend of Richard III's villainy is largely down to Shakespeare, who was writing history for Queen Elizabeth, granddaughter of the victor of that battle, Henry VII. He could hardly do otherwise. Spin-doctoring is nothing that New Labour invented.

At that Battle of Bosworth, slain Richard III's crown fell into a thorn bush, whence Henry VII picked it up and crowned himself. This is the reason for the crown in the bush ironwork surmounting the chapel's north gate.

Henry VII and his son Henry VIII finished the chapel their 15th-century namesake (Henry VII's uncle) had started. Henry VII came to Cambridge in 1506 and had a service of the Knights of the Garter in the finished first five bays, with the uncompleted end boarded over like a film set and decorated with heraldry for the occasion.

Henry's triumph was (apologies to those who don't need this bit of history recapped) in ending the Wars of Roses. He cemented for the first time England together as a unified nation state, by uniting the houses of York and Lancaster. This is evident by the repeated emblem of the Tudor rose, combining the white and red roses of the warring sides, and seen all over the chapel. Incidentally, the very treasure chest in which Henry VII sent some money to the chapel is in the exhibition in the interior, which is thoroughly recommended as a way of understanding the history and construction of the church. Henry VII was an astute politician and realised that by associating himself with this great work of Henry VI, who was then widely venerated as a saint (although not officially), he could give his regime more credibility and legitimacy, and thus stability.

Henry VIII had the chapel finished and, as usual, tried to claim most of the credit. He did provide the magnificent **screen** of dark oak which divides the choir from the rest. This is typically inscribed with many egotistical reminders of who paid for it. HR stands for Henricus Rex, and RA for Regina Anne, or Queen Anne (Anne Boleyn), or sometimes entwined HA for both of them. This puts the screen in the thousand days between his taking her hand in marriage and having her head hacked off, so it must have been made between 1533 and 1536.

This means it was completed just as the shattering effect of the Reformation was sweeping away England's 1,000-year history of monasteries, nunneries, convents and abbeys (Ramsey Abbey, nearby, was pillaged to provide stone for King's and other colleges in an early example of recycling). The screen, however, was part of the Roman Catholic tradition of not letting the lay congregation see too much of what went on at the altar – many a church had a rood screen halfway down – and, of course, the services were in Latin. The Protestants, on the other hand, believed everything should be open, in English, the churches plain and unornamented. So the screen was outmoded as soon as it was finished.

The process of Reformation which Henry started came to a head in the following century when Puritan zealots (backed by the increasing power of the middle classes who had become prosperous on the backs of the monastic land carve-up and resented the king taxing them without asking) not only chopped off the head of King Charles I but also chopped off the heads of many statues in English churches.

They sent out commissions to smash stained glass and graven images, which they perceived as idolatry, and they were deeply opposed to what they saw as superstitious worship of saints and veneration of their relics. King Charles I, by the way, clearly had a new gate added to the screen, for his arms are above the doors and the date 1636 is shown there.

One such commission was sent to Cambridge to enforce the rule of these intolerant, humourless and bossy zealots (the politically correct of their day, one might mischievously suggest), yet somehow the massive stained glass of King's Chapel (which, after all, represented three things they hated – royalty, a saint and ornament) was not smashed.

No-one really knows why, although one contemporary records Roundhead (that is Republican, Puritan, Parliamentary and anti-Royalist) troops stationed in Cambridge and using King's Chapel for their parades and exercises during bad weather.

You can see something of the impact of those beliefs in the figures of saints in the doorways into side chapels which have their faces smashed off. This also happened at Oxford, where a statue of the Virgin Mary holding the infant Christ, too high to reach in the porch of the church of St Mary the Virgin, received a bullet from a Parliamentary soldier. Charming.

In World War II, which saw many a church burned out through German bombing, precautions were taken against the windows being blast damaged, but the chapel was spared again.

That this King's College Chapel, which tells in its fabric so much of England's turbulent and fascinating history from the Wars of the Roses to the Civil War, has survived all that hatred and violence so intact is a miracle in itself.

A VERY BRIEF GUIDE To save you the expense of buying a guidebook on top of the considerable cost of admission (although you may wish to buy a guidebook anyway as it has some superb photographs, and makes a good souvenir, and you can get in without charge, as explained at the end of this section), I would say read the above sections first. They contain a commentary on the **fan vaulting** and the **screen**. It is possible to join a guided tour group and this is usually worthwhile. If so, contact the Cambridge tourist office (☎ *01223 331212*).

Assuming you are using this guide, the symbols to look out for are the Tudor rose, emblem of the Wars of the Roses being ended in unity; the crown and portcullis for kingly authority; and Henry VII's arms combining the greyhounds of his mother's family and the dragon of Wales for his father. Note how the greyhounds vary, deliberately, along the walls.

The stained-glass window, as often written elsewhere, was a form of medieval visual

GARGOYLES

Gargoyles, creatures which form a significant part of Cambridge's population, are a deeply eccentric part of architecture.

They are subversive, mocking, counter-culture. Sometimes their themes are religious, sometimes they merely send up the great and the good of the day in a form of caricature.

They are renewed from time to time, otherwise their features would crumble into vagueness over the centuries.

Some say their job was to scare away devils heading for the buildings, in which case the two different gargoyles of Prince Philip around the country would seem, well, a controversial choice. In truth, these two are in the subversive cartoon-in-the-sky tradition that would see powerful bishops lampooned in stone on their own churches.

But gargoyles have a serious job of work to do, too. Pedantically speaking, a lot of what people call gargoyles are in fact grotesques, in that they are just carvings without the waterspouting job that makes them true card-carrying gargoyles.

If you climb a church tower and see a pukkah member of the species from above, you can see the stone or lead channel down their backs to their mouths which makes them gargoyles (that vomit, or gargle hence gargole, water), unlike the other statues without such spouts looking down from roofs all over Cambridge which are really grotesques.

Their job, before downpipes and guttering became more widely used, was to carry the water clear of the walls and then spew it out (and those walking below can go to the Devil).

The huge eaves of East Anglian thatched cottages do the same job, for the cob walls would soon crumble if continually soaked. Hence the line in the soil a couple of feet out from the walls – the 'eaves drop' – and it wasn't until I stood within such a line sheltering from a summer shower and could clearly hear everything said within the cottage that the verb to eavesdrop became clear in its origin.

Back to gargoyles. That would seem to explain why the creatures depicted by them always have such long necks, whereas the grotesques can be dumpy, almost flat.

That brilliant writer Terry Pratchett has the gargoyles acting as spies for the city authorities and snacking on passing pigeons, an act which I have never seen in Cambridge, although you can imagine their necks craning this way and that (particularly those hungry ones at the top of Senate House Passage).

But you can see one being used to settle a 450-year-old score. When Magdalene College redeveloped an old wharf into the Quayside Centre in the 1980s a peculiar detail was specified – a particularly ugly gargoyle of a banker, Benedict Spinola, who cheated the college of its endowment in 1574.

He is now condemned to show his ugly face for all time and dribble water into the Cam like a fool. This shows that gargoyles can have something to say. That people called Benedict can be iffy. And that Cambridge colleges have very, very long memories. Revenge is sweet … even after more than four centuries.

aid – particularly when the congregation couldn't read and the services were in incomprehensible Latin. That can't have been the case here, however, and the windows which were completed in the mid 16th century are more a tribute to the faith – as is the whole chapel, far in excess of the size such a small college would require.

The **windows** are a fantastic work of art and worth studying. The upper parts of the great side windows show the Old Testament stories, the lower ones the New.

The East Window (that is at the further, altar end beyond the screen from the entrance) shows scenes from the Crucifixion. The **West Window** (nearer the entrance) repays examination. It is clearly much later in style and shows the Last Judgement and the Kingdom of Heaven. It is thought that by the time this window was to be filled, Henry VIII was dead and the more extreme Protestants took over with the arrival of the boy king, Edward VI. They hated imagery in churches, and thus clear glass was used, the window not being coloured until 1879.

Christ is sitting in judgement. King (and saint) Henry VI, holding a model of his chapel, is at the bottom of the window, near the centre. In the court of the college outside, there is a figure of religion in the fountain and she, too, holds a model of the chapel, set appropriately upon the Bible.

Don't miss the huge painting above the altar, *The Adoration of the Magi* by Rubens, painted in 1634 for a convent in Belgium but eventually given to the college in 1961. The layout of the altar area was changed to accommodate this massive masterpiece.

Also do not overlook the tiny **Memorial Chapel** on the south side of the choir and the fascinating exhibition in the former chapels on the north side. Your ticket will also admit you to the college's splendid grounds, except during the Easter term when students are supposed to be swotting in peace and quiet (but the chapel is still open).

It is possible to join in evensong at the chapel (Mon–Sat 17.30, Sun 10.30 and 15.30 at the time of writing), in which case you don't have to pay the £4.50 admission charge that mere tourists pay. But you do have to sit down, dress soberly, not use cameras, not bring in badly behaved people and hear the service, if not listen to it. Ideally, one would do both kinds of visit. It is worth returning for the beauty of the sounds and the place being used for what it is intended. Even if you have no faith, would you rather see a steam engine in a glass case, or alive and pouring out power, noise, steam and smoke pulling a train? A clipper ship in dry dock, or cutting through the waves with sails straining to the wind? This place isn't just a museum.

GREAT ST MARY'S

It's not many church buildings that should feel shame, but according to a semi-humorous inscription at **Great St Mary's**, the university church (details of how to climb the tower, see page 161) is one of them.

It is to do with the fact that the church was originally built without a tower. A century later, in 1608, one was added, but the churchwarden of that time, John Warren, fell from the top on the day of its completion.

This explains the verse on a tablet at the base of the tower in a typical 17th-century almost-metaphysical style.

A SPEAKINGE STONE
REASON MAY CHAVNCE TO BLAME
BUT DID IT KNOWE
THOSE ASHES HERE DOE LIE
WHICH BROUGHT THE STONES
THAT HIDE THE STEEPLS SHAME
IT WOULD AFFIRME
THERE WERE NO REASON WHY
STONES SHOVLD NOT SPEAKE
BEFORE THYR BUILDER DIE
FOR HERE IOHN WARREN
SLEEPS AMONGE THE DEAD
WHO WITH THE CHURCH
HIS OWNE LIFE FINISHED
ASSO DOMINI 1608
DECEMBER 17

If you like tombstone doggerel that tells a story, then how about this, still clearly legible in **St Andrew's** church at Chesterton in the north of Cambridge? A tomb states:

Near this Place lies Interred
ANNA MARIA VASSA
Daughter of GUSTAVUS VASSA, the African
She died July 21 1797
Aged 4 Years

Infant deaths were not then uncommon, but Africans certainly were. Note the judgements which would be different today: a 'colour haply not thine own' and, on the other hand, slavery described as 'foul disgrace'. (Haply, however, meant by chance, not happily.) On the whole the monument seems to denote a great love for the child.

Should simple village rhymes attract thine eye,
Stranger, as thoughtfully thou passest by,
Know that there lies beside this humble stone
A child of colour haply not thine own.
Her father born of Afric's sun-burnt race,
Torn from his native field, ah foul disgrace:
Through various toils, at length to Britain came
Espoused, so Heaven ordain'd, an English dame,
And follow'd Christ; their hope two infants dear.
But one, a hapless orphan, slumbers here.
To bury her the village children came.

And dropp'd choice flowers, and lisp'd her early fame;
And some that lov'd her most, as if unblest,
Bedew'd with tears the white wreath on their breast;
But she is gone and dwells in that abode,
Where some of every clime shall joy in God.

You are left wondering, for one thing, how a former slave came here and how his little girl was afforded such a posh gravestone when so many were buried unmarked, and thinking that after more than 200 years we will not know the answer. Oddly, a visit to a library helps: we do know about her father, Gustavus Vassa – we even know his real African name, which most slaves were deprived of, being given their masters' names.

He was called Olaudah Equiano and was kidnapped aged 11 from his village in what is now Nigeria by black African slave traders and sold into slavery. He ended up in Virginia as a slave, probably on plantations. He was then sold to a ship's captain and saw the world. After 16 years as a slave he bought his freedom. He came to England and wrote a book *The Interesting Narrative of the Life of Olaudah Equiano or Gustavus Vassa the African, written by himself.* Published in 1789, four years before this little girl was born, the book with its first-hand insights into being a slave became a best-seller and influenced many people strongly against slavery. Not long after that it was abolished in the British Empire, partly as a result of a man seeing a horse being whipped up the road to Cambridge and thinking this was how slaves were treated (to find the monument, see my book *Eccentric Britain*).

OTHER ECCENTRIC CHURCHES

LITTLE ST MARY'S This church should be of interest to Americans as it holds the tomb of Godfrey Washington, a vicar of the parish, whose family coat of arms was adapted to make the American stars & stripes. Little St Mary's Lane is off Trumpington Street. Another place that will mean something to US visitors – and surely to any visitor – is the American cemetery at Madingley (take the Madingley Road and it's about two miles out of the city).

ST BENE'T'S CHURCH See above in King's Chapel.

THE ROUND CHURCH The Church of the Holy Sepulchre in, logically enough, Round Church Street, in fact fronts on to the main thoroughfare of Bridge Street leading to Magdalene Bridge. This is its reason for being here – it was originally a chapel for pilgrims crossing the river, but later became a parish church.

This round floor plan is very rare, there being only perhaps four in England (one being the Temple Church, off Fleet Street, London, which has gained unwanted fame through the book and film *The Da Vinci Code*). The congregation here has moved to St Andrew the Great so it is today more of a tourist information centre and museum, but is worth visiting for its exhibition and its simple Norman-style decoration. There is a small charge for entry. I say Norman-style because part of the ambulatory (the cloister-like walk around the circular nave) fell down in 1841 and was heavily restored by Victorians (fairly faithfully) and 100 years later a German bomb shattered the east window which has been wonderfully replaced, with an appropriate theme: 'For the healing of nations'.

Round towers, rather than whole churches, are extremely common in East Anglia, the reason being glaciers. They left the underlying stone covered with so much other stuff that the only stone to hand was flint (which is beautiful, strong and long-lasting but pretty difficult to shape). So you couldn't build strong corners.

ELY CATHEDRAL Not strictly part of this book, but the cathedral, known as 'The Ship of the Fens' does cover Cambridge. Absolutely worth a visit, high points including the railway doggerel tomb (see my book *Eccentric Britain*) and the marvellous lantern that lets light into the interior. There is also a Stained Glass Museum here, not sponsored by Windowlene. Superb siting on what was once an isle rising from the fens, and easily reached by road (A10) or rail from Cambridge.

OTHER DEAD ECCENTRICS

Beautifully lettered in hand-cut italic script and still in perfect condition at **Grantchester** is a right enigma: a gravestone around the top half of which runs

We dance round in a ring and suppose

And around the bottom:

> But the secret sits in the middle and knows

Well it obviously meant something to someone, and beats the sentimental doggerel in making you stop and think. It's the memorial to Sydney Cockerell, a most distinguished Cambridge bookbinder and typographer, and his wife.

Not particularly near **St Giles's church**, Cambridge, itself a rather depressing bit of grim Victoriana on Castle Hill, is the St Giles's graveyard, off the Newmarket Road (through some black gates on the left as you leave Cambridge and down a long path), and it holds a dead interesting set of people. Philosopher Ludwig Wittgenstein (see page 103; his grave is a flat, black, shiny tablet so if the grass hasn't been cut, you may have to poke around), *Golden Bough* author Sir James Frazer, Nobel prize winning Sir John Cockcroft and philosopher G E Moore. As they all died between 1941 and 1967, it suggests when the previous graveyard became standing room only.

MOCK FUNERALS

Mock funerals were an occasional occurrence when a popular student was 'sent down' (expelled). The student's 'body' was laid in a cab in a mock coffin, and the cortège made up of many students in funeral attire, including a choir singing hymns,

followed glumly to the railway station, where the coffin was put in the guard's van. One such cab bore the huge banner 'Alas My Poor Brother' as it made its way up Hills Road. Such funerals weren't always gloomy. On other occasions the 'body' was sat up on the hansom cab and the following cabs all had trumpeters playing tunes.

10 Out of Town

The eccentric towns and villages of Cambridgeshire

STRANGE PLACE NAMES, ODD BODS AND HEROES

BARTON Home to eccentric countryside campaigner, erstwhile presenter of the much-loved *One Man and His Dog* TV show and *Daily Telegraph* countryside columnist Robin Page, who says that the heart of the village has died with the 'cultural cleansing' of the English countryside. Page has painted in his book on the subject (*Decline Of An English Village*, priced £18.95) a marvellous picture of his childhood complete with Barton's eccentrics and characters. He argues that the car and the computer are becoming our masters, not our servants, in the pace of modern life. Nor is he alone in noting these changes which have made many villages mere dormitories for people who shop, work and play elsewhere.

Page's view on the Labour Government's hunting ban were perhaps made clear in 2004 when at his wedding one of the bridesmaids was a hunting hound that emerged from the church with a note tied round its neck saying: 'I'm not a fox hound, Mr Blair, I'm a bridesmaid.'

Mr Page was quoted by the local paper as saying: 'I'm just making a point that I take great exception to people who don't understand the countryside telling me and others what to do with their lives.

211

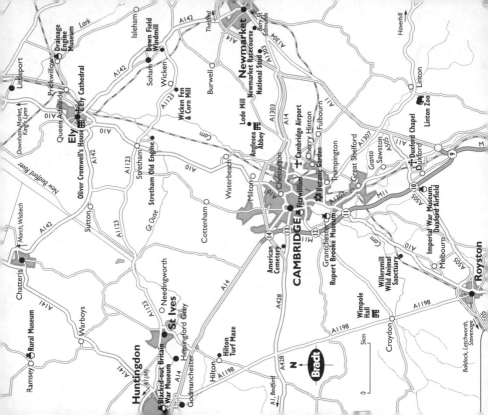

'When there are thousands of dead bodies in Iraq it's amazing that politicians are worried about a few foxes.' Possibly, Mr Page, it's *because* of the dead of Iraq that it's necessary to distract Labour supporters with this class-hatred stuff.

BOTTISHAM Near Stow cum Quy.

GAMLINGAY Julian Clary's betting shop, possibly? Actually a village with a rather good vineyard.

GRANTCHESTER As noted on page 2, the name probably is less romantic and Roman than it sounds, meaning muddy river dwellers. The Blue Ball Inn's name refers to the shock in 1785 when a hot-air balloon flew near here.

IMPINGTON Has an unusual monument to a woman who had a miraculous escape from a giant snowdrift in which she was entombed for a week and a day. On 2 February 1799, Elizabeth Woodcock, a farmer's wife and mother of four from Impington, started back on horseback to the village from Cambridge, where she had been selling produce in the market. The sky darkened and a terrible snowstorm started. She dismounted and led her horse Tinker through the blizzard but the horse panicked and bolted, such was the howling storm. She had cut across the fields to shorten the journey but in the blinding snow and darkness became disorientated and lost. She found a hedge to shelter behind and huddled on the ground hoping to gather

her strength for the renewed battle. She lay there for half an hour and found herself already in a snow cave from which she could not escape. In the morning there was just a slight hummock on the drifts to mark the hedge line in the white, featureless expanse of snow. She was unable to escape, although her horse had made his way home. The family feared the worst as the days went by and assumed the thaw, when it came, would reveal her body somewhere on the way from Cambridge. Meanwhile Mrs Woodcock was trapped in a sitting position. She was alert and could hear the church clock at Chesterton and even the conversation of some passing gypsies on the road. She shouted for help but no-one heard. She could see the moon at night and kept track of the day of the week; she even heard her husband calling for her as he searched. On the night of 9 February William Muncey of Impington had a vivid and detailed dream in which he walked across the fields and found a hare buried in the snowdrifts at a certain bend in the hedge. Then next day he was walking to Cambridge and realised he was at the very spot. He clambered through the snowdrifts towards the spot in his dream and to his surprise saw a red handkerchief moving up and down. Mrs Woodcock had tied it to a stick and poked it through her ice cave's roof. She had also taken off her wedding ring and wrapped it in a nutmeg grater she'd bought at Cambridge market, hoping they would survive if she didn't.

Mr Muncey ran to get help: a horse and cart, blankets and a doctor. She was pulled out but her legs, which had been damp and frozen, were peeled raw.

It seemed she had had a miraculous escape, but her damaged legs caused much pain. Her toes rotted because of gangrene and dropped off and she was bed-bound for months. She died on 17 July 1799. The villagers erected a pillar to her memory in the field where she was found.

HILTON About 11 miles northwest of Cambridge, Hilton has a fascinating turf maze you can follow on the village green (a good picnic spot). This is based on the one in the floor at Chartres cathedral, and like that one (and, in fact, five other surviving British turf mazes) you can see the centre and could easily step over the rings from one to the other, which would be missing the point. This some say is religious, mystic and very ancient, perhaps done on the knees as a substitute for a pilgrimage. In an older pagan version, allegedly, a girl tied to a post at the centre was the prize for boys following the maze (which would give a bunch of Freudians a good day out). Either way, you have to follow the paths to solve it and have the full experience. For that reason, some people prefer the term 'Turf labyrinth'. This one has a pillar inscribed in Latin at the centre: *Sic transit gloria mundi* (thus passes the glory of the world) and further tells that William Sparrow cut it in 1660. As for the *gloria transit*ting, that's a good point: turf mazes only survive while people use them, or else they overgrow. Shakespeare knew this, and in describing a desolate place in winter says:

> The nine men's morris is fill'd up with mud;
> And the quaint mazes in the wanton green,
> For lack of tread are undistinguishable.

A Midsummer Night's Dream, 2, 1

Hilton is off the A14 towards Huntingdon from Cambridge.

Oddly, the largest traditional turf maze in Europe is also near Cambridge, although in the other direction, at **Saffron Walden**. Near the castle ruins, this is about 100ft wide, and dates from at least 1699.

Saffron Walden is about a dozen miles south of Cambridge off the M11 to London (Junction 9), or by train to Audley End (then a walk/taxi/bus of about 2 miles). There is also a grass maze at Cambridge's own Botanic Gardens.

LITTLEPORT This village, near Ely, should be a place of pilgrimage for bikers. One William Harley from this village who emigrated to the USA in 1860 had a son, another William Harley, who met Arthur Davidson, forming, yes, the great Harley-Davidson company in 1903. Mind you, Harleys are better on American freeways than English country lanes and fens round here with their right-angle bends. Uneasy riders, possibly.

MARCH Mad as a March hare could refer to this town in the flat fens where many a hare has been seen or the season when they indeed go a bit bonkers, indulging in mid-air boxing matches, a sight worth catching.

PAPWORTH EVERARD Home of the famous Papworth Hospital, pioneering transplants, formerly the site of the Cambridgeshire Tuberculosis Colony.

PIDLEY It is.

PRICKWILLOW Near Ely, this village is so low in the fen on still shrinking soil that houses have to be built on piles in order to avoid collapse and the dead have to be buried elsewhere because coffins just float in waterlogged graves. Or else put them in above-ground tombs, just as in New Orleans. In fact, they should institute jazz funerals with a bit of voodoo to spice things up. For the museum here, see page 173.

QUEEN ADELAIDE The only Oxford–Cambridge boat race not to have taken place on the Thames was held here in 1944 because of the danger of people gathering in London during the German bombing. It was a dismal day and Oxford won, to make it worse. The place is named after the pub named after the Queen.

REACH Off the B1102 to Burwell northeast of the city. Has an 800-year-old Reach Fair on the May bank holiday which is opened by the Mayor of Cambridge with the national anthem being sung. New pennies are thrown for poor children to scramble for, although whether the children are still poor or whether the pennies are first heated to make them red hot (to make it better sport for the watchers) I doubt. The coins should be £1 pieces to give anything like the original buying power, and the children should be starved for a month or two first. Presumably it was designed to inculcate good old-fashioned moral values. Like what? Stuff the weak, shove 'em out of the way? Cruelty is funny if you're rich? Oh yes, those were the days …

ROYSTON Just over the border into Hertfordshire, Royston is possibly the only place on earth with a newspaper called *The Crow*, an apt choice for a countryside where parliaments of rooks, as the term goes, are often seen in copses of trees with their loud debates and messy mating and nesting habits (not like real MPs, then).

SHELFORD A good proportion of the Cambridgeshire place names are defined by the watery nature of the land, this one meaning shallow ford.

SIX MILE BOTTOM Where Jennifer Lopez came from, possibly. And you thought *your* bum looked big! Not so embarrassing an address as Pratt's Bottom, Kent, however.

SOHAM A small market town, or large village, near Cambridge, is sadly known to some for the worst of human nature. Better here to recall another mainly forgotten and dramatic incident which brought out the very best of mankind: heroism, duty, self-sacrifice and calm professionalism under terrible pressure. It is a story which gives us far, far better reasons for remembering this attractive little town. At about 01.30 on Friday 2 June 1944, a long goods train was chuffing and clanking its unhurried way across the darkened landscape towards Soham from Ely. Although World War II was reaching fever pitch, with the whole Allied effort in top gear for the imminent invasion of Europe, and the buzz-bombs still landing on London, around Soham all was quiet apart from the odd owl hoot and the passage of the train.

People would not have slept so soundly had they known what the goods train contained. Forty-four of its 51 wagons were loaded with 500lb and 250lb bombs destined for an American air-force base. Six more were loaded with fuses, detonators, tail fins and release gear for this fearsome weaponry. All was stacked and roped carefully to prevent mishap and covered with fire-resistant tarpaulins. The signals were clear to allow the train through Soham as it steadily approached.

Something made driver Benjamin Gimbert glance back along his train, although everything had been checked at the last stop. Now Gimbert was horrified to see flames licking up at the corner of the first wagon behind his coal tender. He pulled the whistle cord to alert the guard in his brake van at the rear of the train. Both had the sense not to apply their brakes sharply. Sending stacks of bombs tumbling over would not help, so the heavy train slowed for maybe two minutes to a halt about 200 yards before Soham station.

The driver remained at his post while telling fireman Jim Nightall to get down on the track and run back to uncouple the burning wagon from the rest. He told Nightall to take a coal hammer, in case the coupling was too hot to handle. This uncoupling done, Gimbert opened the regulator as Nightall climbed back onto the footplate and sped the one burning wagon away from the rest of the bomb-laden train. As he passed through the station he slowed to yell to the signalman, Frank

'Sailor' Bridges: 'Sailor – have you anything between here and Fordham? Where's the mail?' He knew the mail train was due and didn't want to endanger another train with his burning bomb wagon.

Bridges was another case of a quick-thinking man doing his duty. He had seen exactly what was happening from his post, had not only made sure the mail train was not yet in that section, but also protected the rear of the stricken train by sending a warning bell to the previous signalbox, and further requested another engine to come and extract the rest of the train. Now he rushed to the platform edge carrying a full fire bucket in a forlorn attempt to douse the flames as the now brightly burning wagon rolled past. But signalman Bridges was never to answer driver Gimbert's desperate question.

A deafening, massive blast blew the wagon to shreds, the 44 high explosive bombs exploding like simultaneous hits from several Flying Fortress aircraft they should have been dropped from. The station was instantly reduced to rubble, the line to a huge crater. Signalman Bridges was killed by the blast, as was fireman Nightall. Amazingly driver Gimbert came round some 200 yards away on the grass outside the Station Hotel where he had been flung. The burnt and bleeding big man staggered, dazed and unbelieving to his feet and asked the startled townspeople who came running whether his fireman and guard were safe. He was kept away from the smouldering crater where his engine had been, and taken to hospital. There, characteristically, he refused to be carried on a stretcher, saying he was too heavy for nurses, and walked in with their support.

Typically for the get-on-with-it era – compared to today where a line is closed for five weeks after an accident – the railway and military, including some US Army engineers with bulldozers, worked like demons to restore the vital rail link. The crater was rapidly filled in and the earth tamped solid, the wreckage removed by breakdown trains and new rails and sleepers rushed forward by willing hands. By 20.20 on *the same day* both tracks were open for traffic again where there had been a gaping pit just hours before.

Soham's station had been completely destroyed and was never properly rebuilt; 13 houses were damaged beyond repair and much of the rest of the town suffered broken windows and lost slates. Several townspeople were injured. Yet had the whole train and all its bombs gone up, had the engine crew merely jumped from the train and run as simple self-preservation would have suggested, or unhitched just the engine to make their escape faster, the whole town would have gone and most of the people with it, leaving just a smoking wasteland. Hundreds would have died.

In the following month driver Ben Gimbert and fireman Jim Nightall (posthumously) were awarded the George Cross, the highest honour the king could give civilians, and the London & North Eastern Railway awarded them silver medals too.

At the time, with the D-Day invasion of Europe going on, their heroism was hardly noticed, with plenty of other heroes dying elsewhere to think about, plenty of bigger bits of history being made.

Eventually all the men involved in Soham's deliverance would be remembered in plaques at the church, and even today you may see two modern diesel freight locos named *Benjamin Gimbert GC* and *James Nightall GC* rumbling around the system, maybe over the very spot. 'They are not the first locos named after those two since the war, nor will they be the last,' said one railwayman.

But for a memorial, who can better the six opening words of the minister at Soham church, also saved from certain destruction, where the villagers gathered on the following Sunday to give thanks for their miraculous escape? As the wind whistled through a few missing window panes blown out by the blast, the minister started: 'But for men such as these...'

STOW CUM QUY Near Bottisham.

WENDENS AMBO Wacky name, wacky people. This pretty little village (two pubs, thatched cottages) on the M11 and main line to Liverpool Street about a dozen miles south of Cambridge has an eccentric habit of celebrating impossible things. Like staging a regatta without any water. Villagers staged their own version by dressing up as boats and 'sailing' up and down Duck Street. They also held a silly air

show with a 'Red Barrows' demonstration and plenty of aircraft noises, mainly emitted by people pushing wheelbarrows, admittedly performing unlikely loops and perfect formations, but, frankly, not many planes. In fact, none whatsoever.

'People who live here have the daftest sense of humour and we are always ready to do something silly,' said a villager. So if you see posters for Wendens Ambo Underwater World or Wendens Ambo Space Launch, be prepared for anything. As for that bonkers name – when the medieval Wenden Magna and Wenden Parva (that is, Big and Little Wenden) merged, they became Wendens Ambo, meaning both Wendens, as in ambidextrous. You knew it would make perfect sense, didn't you?

YELLING Rather quiet.

11 Eccentric Facts

Odd things about an eccentric city and county

THIRTY WAYS OXFORD AND CAMBRIDGE ARE STRANGELY THE SAME

1 Both have a Cowley Road, and both these are slightly disreputable, in a nice kind of way.

2 Both are named after a river crossing, strongly feature rowing and punting, and use blue as their colour (a different blue, true).

3 Both rivers change their names, some pedants say, near the city.

4 Both have Corpus Christi, Jesus, Magdalen, Pembroke, Queens, St Catharine's, St John's, Trinity and Wolfson colleges (any spelling differences being relatively recent distinctions).

5 Both have colleges called Ruskin that aren't part of the main university.

6 Both have a so-called Bridge of Sighs (as in Venice) and both are copies of the wrong bridge.

7   In neither town can you say to a taxi driver: 'Take me to the cathedral' or 'Take me to the university.' They don't exist in the usual sense of a separate location.

8   Both universities use a church called St Mary's instead.

9   Both could have had the railway station in the centre but snootily pushed it out to the edge of town to the annoyance of millions of passengers ever since, but both bus stations are a lot more central. Both have a redundant rail branch line – to St Ives (Cambridge) and Cowley (Oxford) – that should be used but isn't, and a cross-country route that was expensively modernised and then closed (to each other).

10   Both are bicycle mad, being in the flat basin of a river, both being reached through hills that are about 20 miles away from London. Both have had motorways built nearby in recent years, and both have a noisy dual carriageway down the other side. Both have a major airport between themselves and London and a minor one nearby.

11   Both were unimportant to the Romans.

12   Both have remains of pagan well worship.

13 Both were involved in the 1954 four-minute mile and the 1555–56 burning of bishops.

14 Both produced some of the world's greatest children's stories: *Alice*, *The Wind in the Willows*, *The Lion, the Witch and the Wardrobe* (Oxford) and *Winnie-the-Pooh* and *The Water Babies* (Cambridge).

15 Both have many towns named after them in New Zealand, the United States, etc.

16 Both feature a key character called Morse: Inspector Morse in Oxford and Murray Morse, editor of the *Cambridge Evening News*.

17 Both are far away enough from London to be their own place, but near enough for a day out.

18 Both have a saint nobody has ever heard of who turns out to be a defiled virgin with miraculous powers (Frideswide and Rhadegund).

19 Both contain property belonging to the other university.

20 Both contain a place called Paradise.

21 Both had leper hospitals on the edge of town and both retain the chapels of these institutions.

22 Both have an evening paper, a weekly one, and a BBC radio station but not a morning paper.

23 Both have an eclectic mix of museums, some very odd, headed by one huge pile with a huge Neo-classical frontage (the Ashmolean and the Fitzwilliam), plus both have Botanic Gardens. Both have a museum of calculators.

24 Both suffered strife through North v South riots in the Middle Ages, Catholic v Protestant repression and regular Town v Gown head-breaking ever since.

25 Both sets of colleges have long lists of men killed in World War I, both have famous war poets who died in that war, and both have members killed fighting for the Germans, often also listed on memorial plaques.

26 Both have famous university presses and massive bookshops, one of which is unique to each city.

27 Both had technical colleges in the mid 20th century which by 2000 had morphed first into polytechnics and then into the 'other university' in town.

28 Both struggled to cope with the motor car in the late 20th century, banning them from the centre with Park & Ride schemes, despite there being Morris Oxford and Austin Cambridge models.

29 Both have pubs called The Eagle and Child where great people have met and discussed huge ideas (Tolkien, C S Lewis, Crick and Watson). To those who point out the Cambridge one is called just The Eagle, I'd say yes, but only in the last 150 years or so.

30 Both have insanely tall chapels built by the same 19th-century architect who was obsessed by the same 13th-century chapel in France. Gothic revival nut Sir George Gilbert Scott was so knocked out by the Sainte-Chapelle in Paris that he built a soaring version of it here in Cambridge, at St John's, and also in Oxford, at Exeter College. You may think he was right: they're terrific.

CITY ECCENTRICITIES

PEAS HILL The name is nothing to do with the green and mushy vegetable much loved by our friends in the north, and also not a hill, being flat as a mouse sat on by politician John Prescott.

The Peas part might be understood by anyone born in late February/early March. Their star sign would be *pisces*, Latin for the fish and there was indeed a fish market here. And here took place an extraordinary event which would, frankly, be the stuff of folk stories spread by credulous halfwits had it not had top-notch witnesses of the highest standing. On 23 June 1626, a cod that had been caught off King's Lynn by a trawlerman called Skinner was brought to this market by the wife of another fisherman, Mrs Brand. She was selling it when a customer asked for it to be gutted and halved.

The University Bedell, Mr Prime, happened to be also buying fish and saw as the fish was opened a package wrapped in sail cloth was found. Inside, to the amazement of bystanders, was a small book. The Bedell rushed it to the vice-chancellor, who sent it to Boys, the bookbinder, to be cleaned up and put in the library. The book was duodecimo in size (a standard sheet folded into 12, so quite small). In it were three essays: 'The preparation to the Crosse and to Death and the comfort under the Crosse and Death'; 'A mirror or Glasse to know theyself. Being a treatise made by John Frith whiles hee was a prisoner in the Tower of London AD MDXXXII' [1532]; and 'The Treasure of Knowledge.' Who the owner of this book was and what became of him or her – perhaps drowned at sea in which case having read the book may have been indeed of comfort – will never be certain but the words in it became for a while widely known. A reprint of 1627, the year after the fish was opened in Peas Hill, was entitled 'Vox Piscis or the Book Fish contayning Three treatises which were found in the belly of a Cod-fish in Cambridge on midsummer Eue last.'

These were read with great reverence, as if they were the voice of God, rather than the voice of cod. You, of course, may prefer your cod not to have opinions, and

DO CAMBRIDGE STUDENTS HAVE SOMETHING AGAINST AUSTIN CARS?

On 8 June 1958, in one of Cambridge's most audacious pranks, students placed an Austin van on the roof of the Senate House, 85ft above ground. It was never known by whom or how this was done, various theories about scaffolding being advanced. But in those days such vehicles could be unbolted and taken to pieces, which may have played a role. In the event it took ten workmen and several attempts to get the thing down again. As the derrick being used buckled on the second attempt, students watching on the roof of Caius offered the advice: 'Get some undergraduates to do it, they know how.' Which turned out to be not only cheeky but also good advice. In the end it took the authorities days to get it down and they cut up the van in the process.

Students seem to have a thing against Austins. A few years later an Austin car was loaded on to four punts, floated down the river and attached to the Bridge of Sighs at St John's by ropes. The punts were taken away and the car was left there with its wheels a couple of feet over the river to astonish the world. What japes!

It's ironic that Austin was the object of Cambridge students' ridicule in those days. Motor manufacturer Herbert Austin (by then Lord Austin) had done a lot for Cambridge by financing the much-needed Austin Wing (not a spare part, but a building) of the world-

with chips, salt and vinegar. And even with mushy peas, pronounced mooshy oop north, where they are revered and coloured a deeply unnatural green. And the hill class Rutherford Laboratory just before World War II.

Austin was a good engineer (although I once interviewed an elderly former employee of his who recalled Austin resisting hydraulic brakes on all four wheels). Austin cars of the 1920–50s are remembered with great affection by people of a certain age (and collected by younger people, as many still run very well). But in the

changed world after that a forced merger with his hated rival Morris was followed by dire models of indifferent performance, quality and reliability. I know, I bought one in a fit of misguided patriotism. No-one else admits to buying the dreadful Austin-Morris cars of the 1970s and 1980s, it seems: the Allegro, Maestro, Ital, Metro, Maxi, etc. So bad was the build quality in that era that just about none of the millions made are visible on the roads today, and the whole caboodle had gone down the khazi of history by the end of the 20th century.

part of Peas Hill? It meant merely a bit of hard ground compared to the fen-like bog originally all around. In other words, the only bit *not* mooshy.

PARKER'S PIECE This wide open green space between the city and the, er, other university in Mill Road has a Narnian lamppost in the centre, which looms eerily out of the December fog like the one in *The Lion, the Witch and the Wardrobe*. It used to have a graffito on it saying 'Reality Checkpoint' which was apt, because you had lost all contact with the city by then in fog and were steering only by the gleam of this lantern. It serves as a park and I like the way schools, when they want a running track or a sports day, just arrive and mark out a running track on the grass. What I mean is I don't like the bureaucratic types who elsewhere say: 'Oh no, no, no, it's got to be all fenced off. What if we get perverts, children running away, what about dogs? It's got to be a proper fenced-in running track (used for absolutely nothing most of the year).' As Cambridge shows, why? Far healthier to integrate schools and office workers and students in one open space. For the restaurant on the edge of this, see page 141.

JESUS GREEN Site for some unholy goings-on from time to time. For example, in 1646 Goodwife Kendall was hanged as a witch here. The sketchy evidence was that she had been seen on the Sabbath dining with the Devil and speaking strange tongues. This was in the period when those humourless zealots, the Puritans, were in ascendancy and it was enough merely to be denounced by a neighbour, much as people were denounced as Communists in McCarthyite America. Anyway, as the people of Hartlepool once hanged a monkey because they thought it must be a Frenchman, how do we know she wasn't speaking French?

THE SMELLY CAM You wouldn't have wanted to go swimming in the Cam, or punting in it even, until the town gained mains sewerage in the late 19th century. Gwen Raverat writes: 'I can remember the smell very well, for all the sewage went into the river, till the town was properly drained, when I was about ten years old. There is a tale of Queen Victoria being shown over Trinity by the master, Dr Whewell, and saying as she looked down over the bridge: "What are all those pieces of paper floating down the river?" To which, with great presence of mind, he replied: "Those, ma'am, are notices that bathing is forbidden."' As the granddaughter of Charles Darwin further comments in her memoir, there was good reason that the bathing places were on the upper river, on Sheep's Green and Coe Fen. See booklist, page 109.

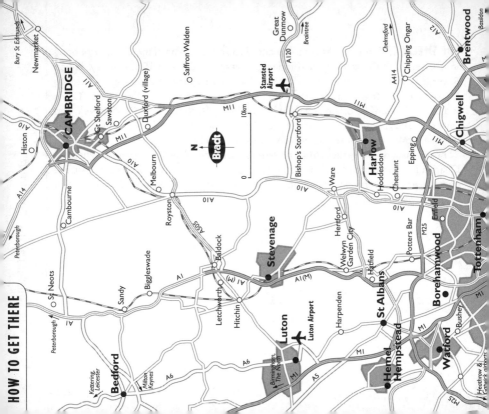

Bury St Edmunds

Newmarket

A11

A10

CAMBRIDGE

A14

Histon

A10

M11

Gt Shelford

Sawston

Duxford (village)

Saffron Walden

Great Dunmow

Braintree

A120

Chelmsford

Chipping Ongar

A414

A12

Brentwood

Peterborough

A14

Cambourne

Melbourn

Royston

A505

Baldock

A10

M11km

10km

0

Bradt

N

M11

Bishop's Stortford

Ware

A10

Harlow

Hoddesdon

Cheshunt

Epping

M11

Chigwell

Enfield

A10

Tottenham

Peterborough

A1

St Neots

Sandy

Biggleswade

A1

Letchworth

Hitchin

A1(M)

Stevenage

A1(M)

Hertford

Welwyn Garden City

Hatfield

Potters Bar

M25

Borehamwood

Bushey

Watford

M1

Kettering, Leicester

Bedford

Milton Keynes

A6

Birmingham, The North

M1

A5

Luton

Luton Airport

Harpenden

A6

St Albans

Hemel Hempstead

M1

M25

Heathrow airports

Stansted Airport

M11

A11

Basildon

A12

12 Nuts and Bolts

HOW TO GET TO CAMBRIDGE

BY ROAD The classic approach to Cambridge by road is from the south. In fact, there are three routes **from London**, all crossing the suburban orbital North Circular Road and the M25 motorway which rings the capital beyond the suburbs.

The first is the original Cambridge Road, the **A10**. It wanders in no great hurry through north London, through Tottenham, Edmonton and Enfield to the M25. It then passes reasonably quickly through a few nondescript towns before eventually turning into a single carriageway road that, dead straight, heads up and down the rolling hills just before Royston, a small town just 12 miles short of Cambridge. Obviously a Roman road, it was known in medieval times as Ermine Street.

Clearly some bossy bureaucrat doesn't want you to use this, as it doesn't mention Cambridge at the M25 London orbital motorway, but it's a decent run and it takes only half an hour to Royston from the M25 on a clear day.

The more modern **M11** runs further east. It's ideal from east London, and the M25's river crossing at Dartford and therefore from Channel ports such as Dover, as well as Gatwick Airport.

If coming from the west of London, northwest London, west of England and Wales, or Heathrow Airport you would do far better to take the **A1(M)** north from the M25 junction 23, turning off after around 20 miles at Baldock (a small but ancient place worth visiting for its broad, handsome Georgian main street stuffed with more cafés and pubs than six normal towns put together, and a useful loo in the town hall at the bottom on the left) and then taking the A505 east towards Royston across open rolling country.

This has the benefit of completely avoiding the risk of terrible jams that sometimes occur on the M25 going clockwise approaching the Dartford crossing of the Thames. It doesn't often happen, but one day when I went to Cambridge it was 25 miles solid, with people stuck in it for eight hours of sweltering heat. Was I glad I'd taken the A1!

As you pass Royston on your right, pick up the A10 (go northeast, that is left) for the last few miles to Cambridge.

From Scotland, the North and the Midlands, use the **A14** from either the junction of the M6 and M1 near Birmingham, or from the A1 much nearer Cambridge, at Huntingdon.

Parking strategies in a city designed to drive motorists doolally: read before it's too late! By all of these routes you can approach the city from the same entry point, and you have to decide very quickly at Trumpington, right next to the M11 junction 11 with the A10 southwest of the city, whether to take the **Park & Ride** bus. This will work out cheaper and, believe me, will probably be a whole lot less hassle than trying to park in Cambridge (you can't drive in the centre anyway, and if you arrive between 07.30 and 09.30 it will be hellish getting anywhere near). The Park & Ride buses run frequently, cheaply and late.

Parking at the **Trumpington Road** site is plentiful and free, there is a tourist information/drinks/toilets place to shelter in, return fares to the city are only £1.80 for adults, and up to three children (under 16) go free per adult ticket. If any city council wanted people to use Park & Ride facilities, this is how they would do it. Clean, cheap, fast, convenient.

The bus drops you off at Emmanuel Street in the centre. Take a note of the bus stop letter (the road's full of them) and hang on to your ticket for the return. Note the last bus time if you're having an evening out. It was 23.15 last year, 22.30 the year of writing, so check.

To reach the city centre and colleges, go back to the end of the road, where the bus came from, and turn right (unless you came via the Grafton centre, in which case go the way the bus was going, then turn right).

Nor is this the only Park & Ride route (you must be careful to board the *correct one* for your return at the same stop you alighted at – see front of bus for destination).

Other Park & Ride routes and how to get to them are:

Babraham Road site For those approaching up the A1307. Take a right turn at the roundabout after passing the Gog Magog Golf Club, on to the Cherry Hinton Road and after about a quarter mile it's on your left. The second left since the roundabout.

Cowley Road site For those approaching from the A10 from the north or the A14 from the west. From the junction of those two roads take the direction towards Cambridge and then after the roundabout take the left lane, which will take you to the Park & Ride facility.

Madingley Road site West of city but of less use to visitors. Accessible only to northbound traffic on M11 (junction 13), so you would surely have used the Trumpington Road site at junction 11, or carried on there if you were southbound! Turn towards Cambridge on A428.

Newmarket Road site Suitable for people coming from the A14 from Newmarket, Thetford and Norwich. Turn off at the junction marked Stow cum Quy and Cambridge, take first left on roundabout at end of sliproad, go straight over another roundabout (well, make an effort to go round it, obviously) and then the Park & Ride is on your right.

All run every ten minutes, offer free and fairly safe parking, take about 15 minutes to get to the centre, and cost only £1.80 in 2006.

...and if you didn't Park & Ride If you *do* drive in up Trumpington Road, however, there are still some options for parking. If you have a car load of people and/or are spending only a few hours in Cambridge, you could aim for the multi-storey car park beside the aptly named Parker's Piece (a park) southeast of the centre, in which case look out for a hexagonal Jacobean drinking fountain thingy (about 20ft high) on your right and there turn right into Lensfield Road. After a few hundred yards, go straight across a major junction with traffic lights next to a huge church spire and look for the car park on the right, opposite the open parkland.

(If you have missed that turn and instead reach the limit of navigation, as it were, for cars, don't panic. Turn right down Pembroke Street and at the far end, turn right and then left at the major junction with traffic lights, opposite a huge church spire, and look for the car park on the right opposite the park.)

The road at the car park is called Gonville Place and the car park is officially called **Queen Anne Terrace Car Park** (595 places, and at time of writing £4 for five hours).

From the car park, cross the road (there is a crossing to your left), walk across the green space, Parker's Piece, to its far left corner and on down Regent Street which leads to the city centre. There are other car parks but they are either small and full, cleverly hidden away down labyrinthine one-way streets, ludicrously expensive for a tourist (the Grafton Centre east car park, £18 for five hours), or insanely far away (the one at the railway station, for example, which is obviously not so insane for a Cambridge person catching a train, just insane for you).

Alternatively, and only if you are heading for just one central thing *for a short period,* such as King's Chapel or a punt from Trinity Boat House, you might get lucky by heading directly for the Backs. So as you come towards the top of Trumpington

Road and notice the aforesaid hexagonal drinking fountain thing on your right, turn left down Fen Causeway, cross the river (amid green meadows) and turn right at the roundabout. Follow Newnham Road for half a mile or so over some more lights until you have leafy green sward on your right under trees and parking meters on that side. Here are a few metered parking places along what is now **Queen's Road**. This makes sense, as I say, only for a short visit, as there is a two-hour limit on the meters (£3 at time of writing) but it is the most amazingly convenient way to get to the Backs of the colleges in a city designed otherwise to send car users into spasms of fury. It is an insider tip you should not let too many outsiders know.

If there are no places here, don't panic, don't panic! Stay on this road as it curves right a bit and then go left at the crossroads and traffic lights up Castle Street. **Castle Hill long-term car park** is after Shire Hall on your right (115 places, £4.80 for eight hours, £2.40 for four hours). If this is full, *do* panic. You should have got the Park & Ride, shouldn't you? Don't you wish you'd gone on holiday to Vulture Gulch, Arkansas, where the only thing that wants to park in the Main Street (the only street) is tumbleweed?

BY RAIL The city is well served by several train companies and routes. At the time of writing there were two operators **from London** (the company names can change, the routes don't). One called First Capital Connect runs from London **King's Cross** (usually platforms 8, 9 or 10, and if it's the latter look for platform 9¾ as in *Harry Potter* on the left as you go through from the main station – you can even be photographed pushing a trolley through the wall. Wizard!). This more or less follows on the A1/A505/A10 route described for roads, the right turn off the main line to Edinburgh coming at Hitchin (so catch the right service) and thence via Royston. Highlight: the immense nine-million-brick viaduct at Digswell, shortly after Welwyn Garden City (the route narrows from four to two tracks just before, so look out then). Journey time: a little less than an hour.

Another company, confusingly called 'One', runs trains from London **Liverpool Street** up another route to Cambridge, via Bishops Stortford. Journey time: a bit more than an hour.

At the time of writing, an adult day return from either London terminus was £17.60 and a Saver Return (for a longer period, but you must start after 09.30) was £25.10.

Cambridge also has direct rail links with nearby **Stansted Airport**, to **Bury St Edmunds** for the east coast ports of Harwich and Felixstowe; to **Ely, Norwich** and branches to the Norfolk coast; to **King's Lynn** to the north, and to **Peterborough**, well served by trains for Scotland, York and the Northeast and the English Midlands. Unfortunately some complete cretin pulled up the direct Cambridge–Oxford line in the 1960s, just after it had been expensively modernised too, so you have to go via London.

Cambridge Station is a fair hike from the city centre but there are frequent buses (right outside in front of the entrance cost £1 in 2006, don't get a return, get off when it turns sharp right into Emmanuel Street, walk back to the road you just turned off and turn right for the city centre). Taxis wait at the station too.

National rail enquiries: ☏ 08457 48 49 50.

From Europe As this book comes into service, so will the **Eurostar** link from Paris or Brussels through the tunnel to London St Pancras. This new route will not only make it a lot faster (186mph) than going via London Waterloo, but also convenient for King's Cross, next door to the new terminus. This will make it quicker than air to Cambridge (city centre to city centre) from these capitals, unless it's to Stansted.

If you are reading this overseas and planning to tour around Britain, consider the **Britrail pass**. You can't buy it in Britain and must book it in your own country using your currency. Only good if you are moving around a lot. See travel agents or internet. There is also a **London Plus** version which includes Cambridge, Oxford, Stratford-upon-Avon, Weymouth, Dover and the whole area in between.

BY AIR If you can choose, make your life a lot simpler by choosing **Stansted Airport** from which rapid train services or a coach link get you to Cambridge in well under an hour. **Heathrow** means battling into London by rail (the Underground is a lot cheaper than the Heathrow Express, although slower, and goes direct to King's Cross which you need) or taking the coach round London (see below). **Gatwick** also means going into London by rail (again local trains may be a lot cheaper than the Gatwick Express, if it's still running). You can book right through to Cambridge including Underground, avoiding three lots of queuing. Note that Thameslink (now run by First Capital Connect) trains from Gatwick give the option of going straight to King's Cross and thus avoiding the hassle of the Underground completely. **Luton Airport** is just hopeless for rail: you could go into London and out again, although for Cambridge I'd take the direct bus (see below). From **London City Airport** take the shuttle bus to Liverpool Street station, then rail.

BY BUS/COACH From London Victoria coach (British for long-distance bus) station (walking distance of the rail station). About two hours, can be more, but make sure you get a direct bus otherwise you may have to wait somewhere ghastly. Typical adult fare: £16, but the offers and grades are complex.

From **Gatwick Airport** Jetlink 717. At possibly four hours, can be tedious. Better to use Thameslink train (now run by First Capital Connect, just make sure it goes to King's Cross, change there for Cambridge). Many services go via Heathrow and Stansted airports, so a long trip. £34.

From **Heathrow Airport** Jetlink 797. About two and a half hours, every two hours. You can get the 787 (as below) but it's slower. £30.50.

From **Luton Airport** Jetlink 787 via Hitchin and Royston. About one and a half hours. £16.

From **Stansted Airport** many Jetlink coach services. An hour or less. £11.20.

The coach station in Cambridge is at Drummer Street. Fares quoted were typical adult returns in 2006.

Coaches are run by National Express (✆ 08705 808080; www.nationalexpress.com).

BY PRIVATE CAR (WITH DRIVER) If there are three or four of you, you might consider a taxi/car service because public transport is so expensive in Britain. **Apt**

Cars (✎ *01223 565048*) were in 2006 quoting £80 *each way* Heathrow/Cambridge plus a small car park fee if collecting from Heathrow. Getting the Heathrow Express/Underground/train from London (admittedly the most expensive option) would cost around £110 *return* for two, so all you need is a child or granny in tow (you can get one at Duty Free!) and the car with driver stops being a luxury and starts seeming competitive (and a lot less hassle.). Unbooked taxis, however, are ruinous.

Note All the above fares, operators and timings are subject to change, and there may be new operators, but the basic route information should stay the same.

TOURIST INFORMATION

The Cambridge Visitor Information Centre is at The Old Library, Wheeler Street, Cambridge (✎ *01223 464732, for accommodation* ✎ *01223 457581, for tours* ✎ *01223 457574*).

TELEPHONE NUMBERS

The 01223 code indicates Cambridge. You don't have to use it within the area but it doesn't matter if you do. Calls from overseas should use your international access code, then the country code (44), then the area code with the 0 dropped off (1223 in Cambridge) then the individual number, probably six figures.

Emergencies 999. Directory enquiries 118 500 and similar numbers.

13 Eccentric Glossary

From Ark to Aegrotat via Glommery to Wranglers

This is your guide through the tangled linguistic jungle of Cambridge University's deeply, deeply strange terminology.

AB What BAs were called until the 19th century. *Artium Baccalaureus* meaning Bachelor of Arts. Ditto AM and MA.

ADC The Amateur Dramatic Club, and its theatre, which has run since 1855.

Aegrotat He (or she) is ill, literally. A type of degree awarded to someone who was too ill to sit the tripos exams. Several of them would be *aegrotant*.

Alma Mater No, not Mike Baldwin's old girlfriend in *Coronation Street*, but the confusion is understandable when you look at her as often depicted in Cambridge. I was once asked at my first proper job interview at an old-fashioned county newspaper about my 'Alma Mater'. I realised it was a test of my education, and I was failing that test. I remembered from school Latin that the phrase could have meant 'soul mother' and guessed, luckily correctly, that it might mean educational establishment. I blathered on about school and college and after what seemed ten minutes, reading upside down noticed the Editor, a fine old man who turned out to be the best employer I ever had, write 'lucid'. Anyway, it's all the fault of the Cambridge University Printer who in 1600 produced a book with a frontispiece displaying the emblematic figure of the university – a woman with large breasts (we're nearly back to *Coronation Street*) on a pedestal with *Alma Mater Cantabrigia,* which means according to Dr Frank Stubbings (see booklist) whose Latin is very considerably more advanced, 'Cambridge our nursing mother'.

The figure holds a sun and a cup into which heavenly drops fall (or she may be projectile lactating on closer examination), with the following caption: *Hinc lucem et pocula sacra* which means 'From here the light and sacred cups', or more freely, 'Hence flow enlightenment and knowledge'. The Alma Mater character was adopted as the emblem of the University Printer from that day forth. In the days of metal type, fancy artwork such as this was the only guarantee against forgeries. Like frilly stuff on banknotes, aces of spades and passports.

Alumnus Pretty well-known word for a graduate, thanks to endless American college films, but actually means in Latin nursling, one who is nourished, which fits in well with Alma Mater (above). In English it means a student who has matriculated, but not necessarily graduated. Plural *alumni*, feminine *alumna* and *alumnae*.

Another place The evil empire that is Oxford, an ugly Midlands car factory with some sort of crummy colleges attached. This aversion to naming your arch-rival is like that in the House of Lords where they must refer to Another Place, not the Commons (or is it the other way round?).

Apostles A society formed in 1820 for the free discussion of any topic. Membership is by election.

Arch & Anth A dotty old couple who lived in Royston. Also, Archaeology and Anthropology.

Archimedeans The Cambridge University Mathematical Society. Journal: *Eureka*.

Ark The Museum of Classical Archaeology, appropriately.

Assizes From 1381 the Bread and Ale Assizes allowed the university to check the qualities and quantities for sale. A source of great friction between Town and Gown.

Austin A building, part of a strange relationship with the eponymous car (see page 230).

Backs Simply the back of the colleges that line the east bank of the river; the area between them and the river or by extension across it to Queen's Road.

Baitsbite to Jesus The normal course for rowing on the Cam, these being names of locks.

Bats Mammals resident at Queens' College. Either the small furry ones in the roof (which fear diarrhoea above all illnesses) or the large less hairy ones in the college's dramatic society.

Bedder A usually female servant in the colleges for domestic cleaning etc. Used to be bedmakers and fetch hot water to pour down the students' backs, making up fires etc. Nowadays more of a cleaner. Once paid almost entirely in tips and unused commons (below) which they would carry off in baskets and resell. The bedder takes on a *staircase* in a college, that is the various *sets* of rooms off one stairway. In Another Place they are called Scouts.

Bedells Surely of a similar origin to Beadle, these ceremonial officials busy themselves with certain formal and legal occasions. There are Esquire Bedells and Yeoman Bedells just to complicate things. The former walk in processions with the vice-chancellor holding huge silver maces with which they would theoretically defend him or her, although I'd like to see one – Michael Heseltine-style – swinging the mace around before braining the attackers. The Yeoman Bedell or Inferior Bedell or Dog Bedell is in abeyance, but he still has a mace which is carried by the Marshall instead, just in case some mad miscreant monkey attempts to assassinate the V-C.

Blue Two meanings, the colour Cambridge blue, which is light blue (Pantone 284 on a computer, I'm told) as opposed to Oxford's dark, and also the honour of competing against that other university in sport. One becomes a Blue rather like one becomes an England Cap for playing for the country. Also some lesser sports (may I suggest, by the way, dwile flonking, bog snorkelling or conkers?) earn a half blue, which sounds like a mauve grey. The people concerned, if multi-talented, can become one and a half blues, an even more peculiar concept. Deep purple, possibly.

Bumps Rowing races in which boats try to bump the ones in front (basically because the Cam isn't wide enough to row alongside each other, unlike the Thames). Involves the occasional sinking and much mockery from the banks.

Buttery A kind of cafeteria cum tuckshop attached to college kitchens where one might eat something other than the formal college dinners. Having had one at school, I'd always assumed it was something to do with butter, but learned Cambridge people point out that, like butler, its origins are probably to do with bottles.

Cat Short for Cambridge Arts Theatre.

Cats or Catz Short for St Catharine's College.

Coffee Rather boringly, the drug of choice for today's so-serious students. In fact, such is Cambridge's obsession with the beautiful, brown-baked berry (not really a bean) that one suspects agents of the Coffee Marketing Board have got together with the spies from Another Place (see above) and hijacked one of the university radiotelescopes to convert it into a Coffee Bar Duplication Ray-Gun, no doubt controlled by some evil bald git in a rotating black leather chair stroking a white cat. If you see one of these enormous dishes being pointed at the city, this is the explanation.

I mean you go into Heffers? Coffee bar. Borders: Coffee bar. Church: Coffee bar. Museum: Coffee bar. Station: Coffee bar. In between these institutions that would make a visiting Costa Rican dance with joy, there are more coffee bars in case you can't stagger 40 yards without another shot. In my day we didn't have *mocha latte gran turismo in excelsis gloria*. (Is that decaff? With Peruvian goat's milk? Skimmed or semi? And unrefined demerara organic sugar or Bolivian natural cane?) We made do with honest, simpler stuff: cannabis, Speed, scrumpy, LSD, opium, brass polish, revolting home-brew beer, vodka stolen from grown-ups, etc, etc. Maybe that's why students are so damned studious nowadays and fewer of them are in mental hospitals. Not that coffee is all good, of course. There was a report when I lived in Cambridge of an undergrad who had not revised much. She sat up all night and ate spoonfuls of dry instant coffee (yeuch) from the jar until she was buzzing. The whole jar! She walked into the exam the next day, scored the highest mark of her life and then dropped dead.

250

Commoner Nothing to do with being a pleb, lout, yob, oik, chav or some such lower order. In fact, many Cambridge commoners are posh, and could be aristocrats or Eton scholars. It simply meant those who paid for their own food (commons, below) rather than exhibitioners and scholars who didn't.

Commons Food eaten in common. Not much used outside Cambridge nowadays except you may hear older people talking about 'short commons' (ie: not enough grub).

Court Used instead of quad, a term from Another Place, for the large square spaces surrounded by buildings. The large square space surrounded by teeth, however, may be Cherie Blair on a flying visit.

Desmond Studentspeak for a 2:2 degree, a Desmond, named after Bishop Desmond Tutu of South Africa. Allegedly.

Dons Slang name for all tutors, professors, masters, fellows, lecturers, etc.

Emma Emmanuel College.

Exeat Boarding school types may remember this term, being permission to leave, or he may leave. Plural is, illogically, *exeats* but, hey, that's what happens when you mix two incompatible languages.

13

Exceedings Special college dinners for certain occasions. What a lovely concept.

Exhibitioner In an academic sense, means a particularly high-scoring student who gets a money grant to help him/her being at Cambridge, becoming an exhibitioner, not necessarily an exhibitionist. Better than a commoner or a sizar, not as good as a scholar. Related to brains, not need.

Fitzbilly Studentspeak for Fitzwilliam, as in museum or college. By extension the totally excellent Fitzbillies bakery and restaurant.

Footlights A student amateur dramatics society, with the accent on satire, which has produced many great actors and humorists.

Glomery There was once a Glomery Hall in Cambridge and a Master of Glomery. See page 116.

Gogs Slang name for the Gog Magog Hills, beyond the far end of Hills Road. These could be considered hills only in the East Anglian context. We're talking Gwyneth Paltrow, not Pamela Anderson here. There is a country park here where Arabian Godolphin, the racehorse from which nearly all others are descended, lies buried.

Graduand Person about to graduate.

Gyp Archaic word for a college manservant, out of use since the last of the species died off in the 1970s. Still exists, some claim, at Girton and in the Cambridge term gyp-rooms, meaning the places where washing-up could take place, brooms and dustpans be stored, etc.

High table The master and dons usually sit at a table in the college hall set at right angles to the main ones, and raised on a wooden platform. By extension the elevated people who would sit at such a table.

Hood Attached to academic gowns for various occasions, these denote rank and learning and are carefully distinguished by colour and design. Insanely, even though Cambridge is the coldest place outside Siberia when the winter wind blows from the north or east, they are never, ever worn. Perhaps to stop people looking like those dead chaps in *Lord of the Rings:* all hood and no face. People actually wearing hoods, on the other hand, are those who the middle class fear are going to steal all their muesli (as if they would be interested): hoodies.

Long vac The long summer holiday. Or a Hoover job in King's Chapel.

Maggie Slang for Lady Margaret Boat Club, ie: St John's College.

Market Hill Flat as a pancake, like Peas Hill.

Mistress Apart from the usual bit-on-the-side meaning, not unknown in Cambridge, the head of Girton College.

Narg Multiple choice: (a) A subatomic particle discovered in Cambridge; (b) A Finnish reindeer milk yoghurt; (c) An exclamation made by someone Turkish stubbing a toe; (d) A Cambridge student who swots all the time, takes studies seriously and has no fun, being an acronym for Not A Real Gentleman; (e) None of the above. Answer: supposedly (d) but I suspect it is (e).

Narnian lamppost Slang for the light in the middle of Parker's Piece, traditionally daubed 'Reality Checkpoint'. Do not *on any account* accept Turkish Delight from strangers beyond here.

Olly, olly A shout of support in rowing races.

Pem & Pot The names for two streams in the runnels or rillets down the side of Trumpington Street along which the waters from Hobson's Conduit run. *Pem* because it goes past Pembroke, *Pot* because it goes past Peterhouse. E M Forster refers to the *Pem* in his book *The Longest Journey* because he has a character called Miss Pembroke. Hobson, see page 50.

Pluck As an examiner, to fail someone at an examination. Shakespeare uses it.

Pothouse Slang for Peterhouse College, apparently.

Proctors Officials in charge of order, supported by constables known as Bulldogs, one of whom, in a pleasing bit of eccentric insanity, would sometimes carry a butter measure. A pair of bulldogs on patrol would always include one sprinter (for quick arrest) and one long-distance runner (for the longer pursuit). This, of course, encouraged students to engineer a chase (such as by not wearing gowns, up until 1960) to try out the bulldogs. The standard fine was half a mark, in medieval times, and this became a third of a pound, which was still a great deal of money. (And if you were one of three brothers often given a pound to share at Christmas, you will know instantly that a third of a pound was 6s 8d. This also illustrates the stupidity of Napoleon's favoured metric system, where you cannot divide a decimal pound into three. Dammit, if we'd wanted decalitres instead of pints, we'd have lost Waterloo, Trafalgar etc. Have you ever seen a case of wine in decimal quantities? Of course not, impossible. Three by four is the natural shape. I rest my, er, case.) To be brought before the proctors was to be 'progged' in student parlance.

Quiche A verb, to try not hard enough, particularly in rowing. They're losing because they are quiching. Derivation: real men don't eat quiche.

Punting A ludicrous, tedious, expensive and accident-prone way of getting from A back to A again on a boat without steering, keel, sides, motor, catering, sails, oars, navigation, GPS, radio or liferaft, and thus extremely popular. Fun to try and a great way to see Cambridge (see page 182).

Rusticate Like squash, has two apparently unconnected meanings at Cambridge. A *rusticated* course of stone in a building is a layer of unfinished, rough-hewn stone in an otherwise smooth wall, for visual effect. A *rusticated* student is one who has been sent down for misbehaving, probably temporarily. The link is in the Latin *rus*, countryside. The one is to build as they do in rural country, the other to be sent back there.

Scarlet days Christmas, Easter and special university days when dons, or doctors in particular, should wear their scarlet robes.

Sets Of rooms, off a staircase. A sort of flat.

Sizar A student who was helped by his college with allowances for food etc. Not related to academic performance but to poverty. Like servitors at Oxford, they used to undertake menial duties to pay their way, but no longer.

Small Bridge The large bridges carrying Silver Street over the River. Great Bridge is the smaller bridge carrying Bridge Street, naturally.

Sophister and sophomores A pointless but, dare I say, fascinating digression that amusingly illuminates our American cousins' great fondness of using the latter word for, I believe, second-year students. *Sophisters*, usually abbreviated to *Sophs*, was within living memory a Cambridge expression used for second-year students who were not yet taking their finals, but not freshmen (first year). The term, now in abeyance, was derived from *sophos*, the Greek for wise. Students today become in turn freshmen, junior sophs, senior sophs, and graduates. However, a writer in the late 17th century humorously described those who were between a fresher and a soph as *sophomores*, the latter half being derived from the Greek *moros*, stupid, foolish, as in moron, and the term stuck for those between wisdom and stupidity. If you like looking at the innards of the language, you will know that sophomore is an oxymoron, a rhetorical device which is sharply contradictory, used for effect. From the Greek *oxus*, sharp, and *moron*, foolish. So a sophomore is half wise, half stupid.

Sporting your oaks A Cambridge phrase which could mean something honours-related like resting on your laurels. In fact, it means the equivalent of those notices on hotel door knobs saying 'Do not disturb'. Sets of rooms in some colleges have two doors, one opening into the room, and one into the hall or staircase. If both are closed (leaving a small gap between them, that is), it means the occupant is away, studying hard and not wishing to be disturbed, discussing Uganda with a member of the opposite sex (or even, fwankly Wupert, the same one), or enduring a hangover from hell after unwisely downing 16 pints of Bogblaster's Old Disgusting at the

Flatulent Ferret last night. A favourite request to departing guests is 'Close both doors, I don't want to be disturbed. Would you mind closing the outer door first please?' According to the learned Frank Stubbings (see booklist), some colleges had a third door in between for extra insulation, which to me seems yet another testament to the coldness of Cambridge, or to the fact that the sinister Secret Guild of Doormakers (motto: 'What use would knobs and knockers be without us?') had infiltrated the university, getting people to fit three doors where one would do being their dream scenario.

Square Correct Cambridge name for the square hat or mortarboard that should be worn by students (if they wear a hat, that is). Mortar boards used by bricklayers and plasterers are still much the dimensions of a Cambridge square, which presumably took its slang name from them.

Squash Either a meeting for freshers in the Michaelmas Term to join certain college clubs or societies, or that racquet game played inside a room where the ball gets squashed.

Suicide Sunday The Sunday after the end of the Easter Term, when exams have been finished but results not known. Students do, regrettably, kill themselves at Cambridge but this is merely a humorous reference to the heavy drinking that goes on then.

Tech, The Name for the former, not to say jumped-up, technical college that gradually morphed into CCAT, then Anglia Polytechnic University, and now Anglia Ruskin University, somewhere beyond the Narnian Lamppost.

Tit Hall Supposedly a nickname for Trinity Hall, although has anyone actually heard it being so used? Yes – frequently. Without causing titters.

Trinners Slang for Trinity College among a certain kind of rugger-bugger undergraduate, probably now an endangered species.

Tripos The name for a Cambridge degree exam, unique to this university, which you might reasonably guess suggests a three-part paper of some sort, a tripartite arrangement. You would be reasonably wrong. Eccentrically, it refers to a Fool on a Stool who made a fairly pointless or satirical speech at examination time, the link being that the stool was three-legged (as indeed is a tripod even today). Of course the thing had a serious beginning, the examinations of students from early times until the 18th century being oral, and taking the form of a disputation between the candidate and an opponent who sat on the three-legged stool, thus known as Mr Tripos. This Mr Tripos attempted to lampoon the students' arguments, and became known for his satire and wit. Later the satirical verses and lampoons associated with the tripos were printed separately, while Mr Tripos and his stool took no part of increasingly serious and written examinations, and even the

Tripos's Latin verses stopped entirely in the late 19th century while the name was kept for the exam. The return of the Fool on the Stool might liven up the more tedious exams today. You can reflect on the pointless name as you sit on a four-legged chair outside a Cambridge café, for it will probably wobble, whereas a three-legged tripod never will, as photographers know well. A digression too far – which I shall, as usual, take – is to say that a good English village is said to be like a milking stool, for it may have four legs, the church, the shop, the school and the pub. It can lose one and stand well, but to lose two is a calamity. I thought this very apt – until I saw a one-legged milking stool being used perfectly well in Ireland. Bgorrah! Give the chap a tripos!

Trivium The only three ways (in Latin) to start a degree in early times: Grammar, Logic and Rhetoric. But it was elementary undergraduate stuff, hence our word *trivial*.

Up and down Let's get one thing straight. You go *up* to Cambridge, even by the *down* train from London. Conversely, you'd catch the *up* train to go *down*. If you got sent *down*, it'd be *down* to what you got *up* to, and you'd certainly be *up* for a dressing *down*. If you went to study a further degree at Oxford, you could be going *down* and *up* at once. You may, of course, be not *up* yet and feeling a little *down*, *down* to *downing* a few pints at *Downing*, which is *up* to you. It all makes perfect sense, like people going *up* the *Downs* in Sussex, or being *down* on your *uppers*, or cricketers who are *in* going *out* and then coming *in* when they're *out*. If you're foreign, you probably think by now I'm absolutely barking. Not literally barking … oh, never mind. It's just the rather flexible English language where it seems a word, as the Red Queen said in *Alice*, means what I want it to mean.

Wooden spoon This now common phrase for a figurative award to he or she who comes last in anything – used in sports reports the world over – recalls the real wooden spoon which was lowered from the gallery at the Senate House as the very last maths degree was awarded. It used to be, in fact, a malting shovel, and it was traditionally inscribed with the name, date and college arms of the recipient (rather as oars are still emblazoned for rowers). The Wooden Spoon and its holder were carried round the town as an honour for being the dunce of the degree. At times the Wooden Spoon was a massive ornamental thing 5ft long, and was dangled twisting over the recipient like the Sword of Damocles. Some are preserved in colleges, such as St John's, which has the last, awarded in 1909 and inscribed in Greek. See Wrangler (next) for the opposite.

Wrangler Nothing to do with the denim jeans, but the term for those who achieve first-class honours in maths at Cambridge. The second-class honours are senior and junior optimes. The highest mark of all goes to the **Senior Wrangler**, an honour indeed.

I say nothing to do with jeans, but there is a link, just about. *Wrangle*, a German-derived word, has two meanings in English. To wrestle with and dispute in the hope of overcoming (presumably the origin of wranglers at Cambridge and an intransitive verb, you wrangle with somebody, you don't wrangle somebody) and an American transitive verb, to wrangle cattle (again wrestling to overcome them, hence a cowboy term, a cattle *wrangler*). That must be where the jeans and the Jeep Wrangler car come from.

WIN £100 CASH!

READER QUESTIONNAIRE

Complete and return this questionnaire for the chance to win £100 cash in our regular draw

(Entries may be posted or faxed to us, or scanned and emailed.)

Your feedback is important. To help us plan future guides please answer all the questions below. All completed questionnaires will qualify for entry in the draw.

Have you used any other Bradt Guides? If so, which titles?.................

....

What other publisher's travel guides do you use regularly? ....

Where did you buy this guidebook? ....

What was the main purpose of your trip to Cambridge (or for what other reason did you read our guide)? eg: holiday/business/charity etc. ....

What other destinations would you like to see covered by a Bradt guide?

....

Would you like to receive our catalogue/e-newsletter?

YES/NO (please give details)...

If yes – by post or email? ....

Your age   16–25 ☐   26–45 ☐   46–60 ☐   60+ ☐

Male/Female (delete as appropriate)

Home country ....

Please send us any comments about this guide or other Bradt Travel Guides ....

....
....
....
....
....

**For a current list of titles and prices, please see our
website – www.bradtguides.com, or call us for a catalogue.**

Order Form

Please send me one copy of the following guide at **half the UK retail price**

Title   Retail price   Half price

. . . .

Post & packing (£1/book UK; £2/book Europe; £3/book rest of world)   . . . .

                                                                      Total   . . . .

Name . . . .

Address. . . . .

Tel . . . .   Email . . . .

☐ I enclose a cheque for £. . . . . made payable to Bradt Travel Guides Ltd

☐ I would like to pay by credit card. Number: . . . .

Expiry date . . . . . . / . . . . . . 3-digit security code (on reverse of card) . . . .

☐ Please add my name to your mailing/e-newsletter list. (For Bradt use only.)

☐ I would be happy for you to use my name and comments in Bradt marketing material.

Send your order on this form, with the completed questionnaire, to:

Bradt Travel Guides/EccCAM
23 High Street, Chalfont St Peter, Bucks SL9 9QE
☏ +44 (0)1753 893444   f +44 (0)1753 892333
e info@bradtguides.com   www.bradtguides.com

Index